The

ULTIMATE
MIDDLE SCHOOL
SURVIVAL GUIDE

Books by Erica and Jonathan Catherman

The Girls' Guide to Conquering Life
The Girls' Guide to Conquering Middle School
Raising Them Ready

Books by Jonathan Catherman

The Manual to Manhood
The Manual to Middle School
Guiding the Next Great Generation
Becoming the Next Great Generation

The

ULTIMATE
MIDDLE SCHOOL
SURVIVAL GUIDE

"Do This, Not That"
LIFE SKILLS FOR SUCCESS

JONATHAN AND ERICA
CATHERMAN

Revell
a division of Baker Publishing Group
Grand Rapids, Michigan

Published by Revell
a division of Baker Publishing Group
Grand Rapids, Michigan
RevellBooks.com

Printed in the United States of America

Library of Congress Cataloging-in-Publication Data
Names: Catherman, Jonathan, author. | Catherman, Erica, 1975– author.
Title: The ultimate middle school survival guide: "Do this, not that" life skills for success / Jonathan and Erica Catherman.
Description: Grand Rapids, Michigan : Revell, a division of Baker Publishing Group, [2024] | Includes bibliographical references.
Identifiers: LCCN 2023031288 | ISBN 9780800745752 (paperback : alk. paper) | ISBN 9780800745769 (casebound) | ISBN 9781493445370 (ebook)
Subjects: LCSH: Middle school students—Life skills guides—Juvenile literature.
Classification: LCC LB1135 .C38 2024 | DDC 373.18—dc23/eng/20230818
LC record available at https://lccn.loc.gov/2023031288

The authors are represented by the literary agency of Books & Such.

Baker Publishing Group publications use paper produced from sustainable forestry practices and postconsumer waste whenever possible.

24   25   26   27   28   29   30   7   6   5   4   3   2   1

WELCOME
TO MIDDLE SCHOOL

YOU MATTER
YOU BELONG HERE
YOU CAN DO THIS

CONTENTS

INTRODUCTION

Congratulations, you've made it to middle school! Gone are the elementary days of line leaders, bathroom buddies, and classroom pets. Instead, you have graduated from avoiding playground cooties to riding the roller coaster of emotions, friendships, and physical changes we call middle school. The ups, downs, twists, and turns during these few years of life can, at times, feel overwhelming to the senses. Kind of like the weird feeling you get at an amusement park when a ride barrels down the track at Mach speeds into a massive blind drop, followed by two loops, and then a stomach-churning corkscrew. Sometimes you feel like you're about to lose your stomach and find yourself screaming uncontrollably. One turn later and your hands are raised high and you're cheering out loud. Guess what? Those are often totally normal feelings in middle school too. Whether you enjoy the thrill of the ride or absolutely hate the suspense, it's best to embrace the changes and learn some new levels of self-control in order to make the most of the next few years. Who knows? You may actually have a pretty good time in middle school.

Jump from the craziness of the amusement park ride known as middle school to the drama of the tweenage theater. A poorly performed "drama" can ruin some potential good times in middle school. The truth is, you may not be able to control all the events that happen around you in middle school, but you *can* decide not to get all caught up in them. Getting involved in middle school drama can be like tossing fuel onto a fire . . . things get hot! Making much to-do about nothing is the fuel that feeds the fire between people and can melt friendships down. Try to extinguish any drama before it starts by thinking carefully about your actions and the words you choose to use in middle school. Here's a good filter: Before you speak, text, or post, pause and *THINK* about what you are about to do or say.

Is it *TRUE*?
Is it *HELPFUL*?
Is it *INSPIRING*?
Is it *NECESSARY*?
Is it *KIND*?

This is the best pro-you and anti-drama hack ever. It's been around for years and works pretty well for anyone mature enough to *THINK* about discovering and developing the best version of themselves in middle school.

We're just getting started. This book is all about giving you lots of helpful hints and the kind of "Do this, not that" advice every kid needs as they grow older. Basically, you want to succeed. And we want you to succeed in not just surviving but better yet—*thriving*—in middle school. For now, please accept this book as our gift to you because we believe in you. We hope what you read next will help you be and do your very best at this age and beyond. Good luck and enjoy your adventures in middle school!

1ˢᵀ DAY

Before you arrive for the first day of middle school, it's best to know a little about what you're stepping into. Here's what you need to know about the first day. Just like you, a lot of the students are new to the building. They are also feeling a little nervous, just like you. The older kids are excited to see their friends, so they won't pay much attention to the new kids walking around. The building is bigger, halls are louder, and passing between classes can be like moving through a crazed herd of cats. The truth is, you might get lost once or twice on the first day of school. But don't worry about it because you won't be the only one. A right turn down the wrong hall can send anybody into the land of the lost. If you do find yourself wandering around, don't freak out. Your best plan for getting back on track and heading in the right direction is only three steps away.

STEP 1—Ask for directions. The worst thing you can do is keep standing there looking lost.

STEP 2—Get moving. The classroom isn't coming to you, so don't just stand there.

STEP 3—Don't make excuses. When you do finally make it to class, just tell the teacher that you got lost. They'll totally understand when you're honest about a mistake.

POP QUIZ

Q: Where is the school gym?

A: You have no idea, so tape a school map on the inside cover of a master folder. When you get lost, just open the folder, read the map, and find your way to gym class.

ABSENCES

According to experts in middle school attendance offices everywhere, there are three legit reasons to be absent from school:

Reason #1, Sick—An infection, affliction, or disorder that can be diagnosed. Symptoms include a high temperature, chunks hurling out of either end of your digestive system, broken bones, or another verifiable illness. NOT sick is when you are faking it.

Reason #2, Emergency—Situations requiring immediate action, like the passing of a family member, your home being damaged in a freak weather storm, or an actual zombie apocalypse. NOT an emergency is the death of your goldfish, "dating" breakups, or your favorite jeans didn't get washed due to a false call on that zombie apocalypse thing.

Reason #3, Professional intervention—When serious life or legal needs require outside professional or legal help. These may include, but are not limited to, counseling, court, or a doctor appointment. NOT an intervention includes "doing time" on the beach or a 10-hour therapy session with "Dr. Pillow."

When you are absent for a day or two, complete the school's online absence form or return to class with a parent's or doctor's note with a legitimate explanation of your absence.

> Don't pretend to be sick and stay home to get out of a test or project. Fake absences still mean making up class and homework when you come back. There goes all your free time for a couple of days.
>
> —COLE C.

ANNOUNCEMENTS

Each morning a mystical voice from the great beyond will guide you into the school day. Actually, the voice will come from a squawking overhead speaker or live-screen broadcast from a "studio" somewhere in the media center or main office. Either way, the info shared over the school announcements is worth paying attention to if knowing today's lunch menu, the bell schedule, the next awards assembly, or the grade level winning the school-wide fundraiser is important to you. Such information is power, so sit down, listen up, and collect all the news you need to rule the day.

TRUE STORY

A true pioneer in media broadcasting is the late, great Barbara Walters. The first female co-anchor of a US network evening news program in 1976, Barbara Walters was featured nightly on the *ABC Evening News*. She earned $1 million a year, which was a first for a female journalist. As one of the most respected journalists in television history, she was celebrated for her interview style and quality, which granted her access to some of the world's most famous and influential people. Listed as one of *TV Guide*'s "50 Greatest TV Stars of All Time," she interviewed movie stars, athletes, heroes, and every US president and first lady from Richard and Pat Nixon through Barack and Michelle Obama. Barbara Walters retired in 2014 after 65 years working as a journalist.

ASSEMBLIES

The freedom of assembly is an important part of the First Amendment to the United States Constitution. When the Founding Fathers penned the rights of our nation, they stated that the people are allowed peaceful assembly. Never did they imagine packs of wild students swarming in crazed assembly. Pep rallies, awards presentations, talent shows, and guest speakers are all perfect times for the entire school to get together and have some fun. The freedoms students get to experience in assemblies include laughing, learning, clapping, cheering, and being part of stuff like class competitions and fun games. Sleeping, messaging, pushing, pranking, and disrupting an assembly are not freedoms, are not protected, and will not be tolerated. So enjoy the break in the school day, keep the gathering peaceful, and the school will grant you the freedom to assemble in another assembly soon.

TO DO IN MIDDLE SCHOOL:

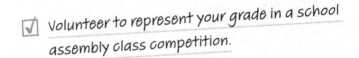

☑ Volunteer to represent your grade in a school assembly class competition.

BACKPACKS

Most schools allow students to carry some of their books and class supplies in a midsize backpack. This reduces your need to stop by your locker between every class and makes it easier to carry stuff between home and school. Some students get the wrong idea about how to use their pack and overstuff it like they are on a yearlong wilderness expedition. Other kids rarely clean out their packs. Old food and sweaty gym clothes quickly go rotten, turning your tote into a putrid canvas petri dish. Your best bet is to pack light and keep it clean. Your back muscles—and the nose of the kid walking behind you—will appreciate it.

STRANGE but True

Experts recommend a student's backpack weigh no more than 10–20% of their body weight.[1] Yet on average, 6th graders carry backpacks weighing 18.4 pounds. Incredibly, some student packs weighed in as heavy as 30 pounds! What are they stuffing in there? Is math class meeting on the summit of Mount Everest?

BATHROOM

Keep It Clean

There are only a few good reasons to visit the room of thrones, and none of them include trashing the place on purpose! Seriously, do what you have to doodoo, if you need "two," but keep it clean. Flush from your mind any urge to mark a stall door, clog a sink, or scratch the mirrors before returning to class.

STRANGE but True

Most people "visit" the toilet 6 to 8 times a day. That adds up to an average of 2,555 times a year. At about 2 minutes per stop, the total is just over 85 hours a year of bathroom usage. Divide those 85 hours of toilet time by 24 hours in a day and wow! You spend almost 4 full days per year using the toilet.

BATHROOM

No Loitering

When you tinkle, you sprinkle, and while in the stall, don't touch the wall. The truth is, there's no escaping germ exposure in the bathroom, public or private. This is bad news for germaphobes and grungies alike. With every "use," particles of fecal bacteria go airborne and land on the floor, walls, and your hands. It doesn't even matter if you're a "foot flusher," nobody gets away germ-free. To make it simple for all to understand, every time you "go," particles of pee and poo stick to you.

The solution is simple. NO LOITERING! Limit your exposure to toxic toilets by not staying and talking in the bathroom. That, and always, always, always wash your hands before leaving.

And PLEASE use soap!

Just Joking

- **You never really appreciate what you've got until it's gone.**
  Toilet paper is a good example.

- **What did one toilet say to the other?**
  You look flushed.

BODY ODOR

Imagine raising your hand to ask the teacher for a bathroom pass. Suddenly your nose picks up the foul scent of body odor. In horror you realize the pungent perfume is your own personal brand of armpit aroma—a.k.a. BO. But it's too late. Before the recoil of your arm can close the pit door, an invisible stink cloud has escaped into the air.

"Who will smell me?" you ask yourself.

"The popular kid to my right? Please no!" you beg in a silent prayer.

"Maybe nobody will notice," you hope in vain.

But then you hear it. The student sitting directly behind you fakes an attention-getting gag as they hold their nose and point in your general direction.

Rewind . . .

There's no need to sweat it. You can raise your hand high with the sweet smell of confidence if you simply shower daily and apply a few swipes of antiperspirant or deodorant to your clean, dry pits. Who knows whose nose will thank you first—yours or the people sitting all around you?

HOW TO . . .

Apply Deodorant or Antiperspirant

Preparation—After showering, dry your armpits.

STEP 1—Remove cap from deodorant. Peel off any product seal from the stick of antiperspirant or deodorant.

STEP 2—Raise one arm. Lift your arm over your head to expose your open, dry armpit.

STEP 3—Apply the deodorant. Swiping up and down in even strokes, apply the deodorant to the skin in your armpit. Repeat under your other arm. Two or three strokes should ensure complete coverage. Too much and people will smell your deodorant before they see you.

STEP 4—Dry time. Before putting on a shirt, allow a minute for the deodorant to dry so it won't leave a visible mark on your clothing.[2]

BOOK REPORTS

You are but one person, writing one paper, in a class of 20 students, all with the same assignment. Your teacher is but one person, grading each paper, from 20 students, all with different perspectives. How will the teacher ever know if you truly read the book? It's just so much easier to skim a few pages, rephrase the book's description, and search the internet for some "ideas" that can be copied, cut, and pasted. Well, believe it or not, teachers know the difference. Maybe it's because they are trained professionals with a degree and official certificate to teach the very class requiring a book report. Maybe it's because they've read way more papers than you'll ever write, and they can smell a false book report a mile away. Your best plan is to do the right thing and actually read the book. Think ahead, pace out the pages, take notes, and draft a real report that reflects what you discovered. Who knows? You might just surprise yourself and enjoy the read.

LOOKING BACK

Writing a book report takes time and attention to detail. I found it helpful to first make an outline of what was required in the book report and then add in details to complete the report. Use your own words to build detail, and be sure to cite your sources and references. Then edit, edit, edit . . . yes, at least three times!

—ERICA CATHERMAN

BRAGGING

It's not bragging if you actually did it," many people say proudly. Yeah, but how many times do you need to tell us you did it? Once is cool. Twice is good. Three times or more and now you're boasting. If you're really that good, then others will talk about you for you. Try this instead. Be interested in other people's interests and accomplishments first. Then when they feel understood and appreciated, they just might ask you about your accomplishments.

Just Joking

A young kid sitting next to an older person brags, "I have over 1,000 friends on social media that I've never met." The older person looks at the kid and says, "When I was your age, we called them imaginary friends."

BRUSHING YOUR TEETH

Everybody likes a friendly smile. Go ahead and show us your pearly whites. Your chompers, your fangs. Most adults' mouths hold 32 naturally off-white teeth. You may still lose a few in middle school, but basically the grill that makes up your grin is the one you'll want to keep for life. This means brushing your teeth every morning and evening, at least. Brushing *with* toothpaste for about two minutes removes food particles and plaque and helps prevent tartar, gum disease, and halitosis. Hal-i-to-sis is the technical term for bad breath from a dirty mouth. Breathing out of a dirty mouth is also called stank, yack chat, and the breath-o-death. Failing to brush your teeth produces a smell that will tell the people you are talking with, "No, I didn't pass gas; I just exhaled in your general direction." So give your ivory a good brushing a few times a day. Your mouth—and noses everywhere—will thank you.

True OR False?

The tongue is the strongest muscle in the body.

False. The tongue is not just one muscle; it's actually made up of a team of eight separate muscles. This fun fact disqualifies it from all future single-muscle competition. The hardest working muscle in the body is the heart. Yet, fail to scrub your tongue while brushing your teeth, and your death breath might just give somebody a heart attack.

BULLIES

Bullies are like skunks. From far off, they can be avoided. But when one crosses your path, life can really start to stink. So follow your nose and steer clear of the haters. That's all a bully really is, a hater. For some very real reason, they don't like themselves much and are choosing to take their frustrations out on others. Don't be that person. Instead, be kind to everybody. Even the haters? Yes, even the haters. But when you do find yourself on the stink end of a bully's day, don't freak out and draw attention to yourself. Instead, try to stick with your friends and go immediately to talk with an adult you trust—like a teacher, advisor, or school administrator.

 Ask a Middle School Survivor

Q: I just know my older sister's friends are going to pick on me when I'm in middle school. How do I deal with them bullying me at school?

A: Sorry to hear about your sister's so-called friends. So, technically, bullying is repeated, unwanted, aggressive behavior that involves a real or believed power imbalance. If your concerns become real and they threaten you physically or play mind games with you, then ask your sister to back you up. Family first! If she won't help you out, go over her head and talk to an adult. You can talk with a parent, teacher, or guidance counselor at the school. Remember, dealing with this kind of stuff is the guidance counselor's job.

—REED C.

BUS

Take Your Seat

I n kindergarten you learned a simple rhyme that went something like this:

> The wheels on the bus go round and round,
> round and round,
> round and round,
> The wheels on the bus go round and round,
> all through the town!

In middle school you'll want to avoid learning a similar song that goes like this:

> The bus driver's head spins round and round,
> round and round,
> round and round,
> The bus driver's head spins round and round,
> when you don't SIT DOWN . . . and zip your lip!

Consider the bus a mobile extension of the school. The good behavior your teachers expect of you in class is also expected of you on the bus. So take your seat, face forward, talk quietly, and always be nice to the bus driver. If someone else is not seated and is continually bothering you, don't put up with it. Tell them to stop. If they don't stop, ask the bus driver, a parent, or a teacher for help.

True OR False?

The bus driver has no real authority to discipline misbehaving riders. Basically, what happens on the school bus stays on the school bus.

False. Misbehavior on a school bus can result in suspension of riding privileges, ISS (in-school suspension), and even criminal charges.

BUS

Waste Not, Want Not

The school bus is not a rolling garbage can. Nobody wants to sit on a bus, period. Absolutely nobody wants to ride in a trashed bus littered with crushed wrappers, ripped paper, old gym shoes, and the rumor of a live rodent named Whiskers that's infected with rabies. So keep your trash to yourself. Keep whatever you bring on the bus *off* the floor, and take it with you when you get off the bus.

Just Joking

What's the difference between a garbage truck and a school bus?

One makes frequent curbside stops, is crammed with bags, and smells bad. The other is a garbage truck.

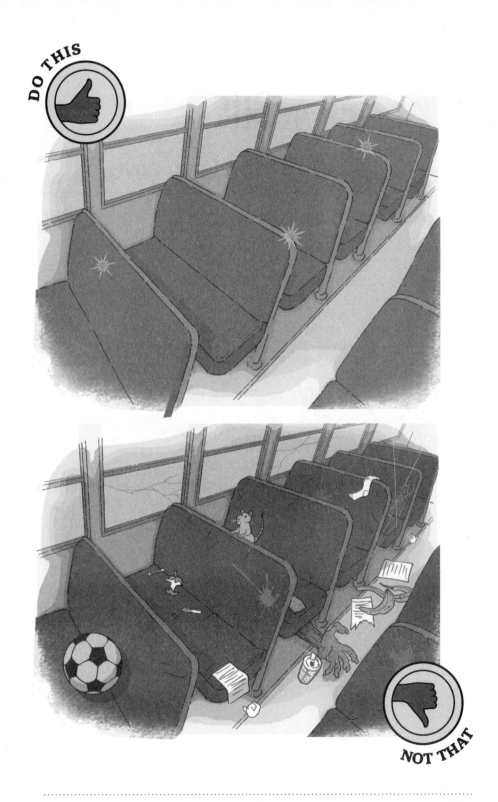

CAR RIDERS

The car-rider pickup line at your school shares one thing in common with its distant cousin the fast-food drive-through line. Both are intended to move cars through a line to a designated point, make a pickup, and speed away in chase of the next commitment in the day. The difference is how long this exchange takes. Drive-through lines have a goal of getting customers in, served, and out in just a couple of minutes. Whereas the school's car-rider line looks more like downtown Los Angeles traffic during rush hour. Parents waiting for students to be released pass the time by snacking, reading, texting, sleeping, and checking social media. Yet both the business drive-through and the chauffeur-like parents must focus on the same goal. Drive in, pick up, and drive out again safely and as quickly as possible.

So do your part and be ready to go when it's your turn to get picked up. Be safe and be quick about it. This way the rest of your day can get started as fast as possible.

Just Joking

Why was the frog waiting at the bus stop?

Because her car got toad.

CELL PHONE

The major organs you need to maintain a happy and healthy life include the heart, lungs, kidneys, liver, intestines, and a bunch of other very important and equally odd-looking body parts. Missing from the list of vital parts is what many middle schoolers consider a required lifeline to their daily survival—the cell phone. Contrary to popular belief, lacking access to a mobile device will not send you to the emergency room nor to the top of the tech transplant list. The truth is, when school rules or class codes exclude cell service, you'll survive. Power it off and put it away, before it gets confiscated.

STRANGE but True

In 1983 the first mobile phone in the US cost a mere $4,000.

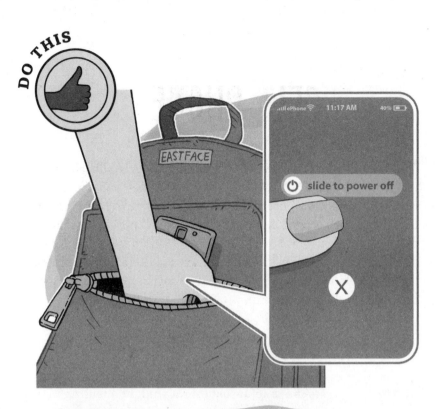

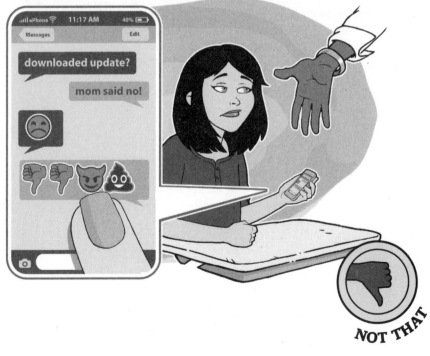

CHEATING

Cheating is easy and for the lazy in life. Thinking the teacher is "dumb" and won't catch you doesn't make the teacher a fool. Instead it shines a light on the fact that you have been trusted with far more than is deserved. Instead of sinking low by cheating, hold your head high and try something a bit more challenging. Build your character on the foundation of honesty, truth, and integrity. You'll feel stronger, stand taller, and be smarter for it.

 Ask a Middle School Survivor

Q: What happens if a teacher catches a student cheating?

A: When a teacher catches a student cheating, they usually take them aside to talk and give them a zero grade. If it happens more than once, the student is often sent to the office.

—MAYA C.

CLOTHING STYLE

Stand out or blend in—the choice is yours. The style of clothes you choose can make an outward statement of the inward you. Many students in middle school end up dressing a lot alike, and that's okay. Some like the athletic look and wearing basically the same styles as the friends they walk beside. Others will choose a more unique style and try to match their hair color to their thrift-store shoes. Some will choose an outfit one day that is totally different from the way they dressed the day before, and that's perfectly fine. You will see kids wearing everything from sci-fi printed T-shirts to collared shirts and ties, from Sharpie-designed canvas shoes to polished leather boots. From glamour to grunge. Unless there is a standard uniform all students must wear every day, you can expect to see about every style the school's dress code will allow. So experiment with the looks you like and wear each with pride. Just remember, clothes look best when they are not imprinted with wrinkles, are clean both to the eye and nose, and are appropriate for school.

 Ask a Middle School Survivor

Q: What if I only have one or two pairs of shoes? Is this going to be embarrassing?

A: How many pairs of shoes you wear shouldn't be a problem. I know for some kids, their shoes really matter. Still, be sure to keep the ones you have clean and aired out. What's embarrassing is to walk around with dirty, smelly shoes with the laces untied. Also, smile a lot and people will keep looking up at your face instead of down at your shoes.

—COLE C.

> Of all the things you wear, your expression is the most important.
>
> —ANONYMOUS

COMMUNICATION

Communication is a numbers game, and you want to win this game. To win you'll need to manipulate the math. Don't freak out. It's easy. To communicate your way to a win with teachers, coaches, and your parents, do the math so your communication equals 100%:

55% body language = Face people, look them in the eye, and smile.

38% tone of voice = Speak clearly and be respectful—no sarcasm.

7% words = Choose your words carefully and stay away from extreme descriptions like "always," "never," "everybody," and "nobody."

HOW TO . . .

Show You Are Listening in Class

Sit up. Sitting up communicates that you're alert and engaged.

Listen up. Listening to your teacher and other students is a good way to make them feel like what they have to say is important.

Ask questions. Teachers like it when you ask them questions. The trick is to know the right kind of questions to ask:

Rule #1—Ask good questions and expect good answers.

Rule #2—Ask lame questions and you'll get lame answers. (FYI . . . lame questions are intended to distract, disturb, and force the teacher off topic.)

Rule #3—Ask no questions and you'll get no answers.

Nod your head. Teachers are really good at reading nonverbal communication. By nodding your head, it lets them know you are getting what they are teaching.

Track the teacher. To track your teacher means that when they move from one side of the classroom to the other, you keep watching them as they teach. (See "Track the Teacher.")

CRYING

Crying in middle school is an emotional subject. Some people say you need to let your feelings show by getting it all out with a good cry. Others recommend that you need to toughen up and bottle it up. What's clear is the average person sheds tears about 2.5 times a month.[3] These tears range from, "No, I'm not crying. I've just got something in my eye," to full-on "get that kid a box of tissues" sobbing . . . or the "ugly cry." One kid might shed tears because they just compound-broke their leg in a soccer game, while another cries from embarrassment when their YouTube video gets zero views.

If and when you do cry is somewhat up to you, yet keep this thought in mind: Gone are the elementary school days of tears over spilled milk or lost pencils. The middle school rules are simple. If you didn't get your homework done, there's no crying. If you forgot the field trip permission slip again, there's no crying. If it's the last day before your best friend since 1st grade moves across the country, some tears may be in order. If you just learned a beloved grandparent has passed away, the tears will flow. If you do feel like a cry is about to happen at school, go talk with your class advisor or school counselor. They'll work to assist you through whatever you're wrestling with, and for sure they can spare a tissue or two.

True OR False?

Only humans shed tears.

False. All animals with backbones—or vertebrae—shed tears. Humans are the only ones thought to shed emotional tears, although elephants have been reported to shed tears when they lose another elephant or are in grief.[4]

CYBERBULLIES

Almost everybody is digitally connected today. Wired or wireless, a streaming virtual feed of data is available anytime, from anywhere, between any people. This means flesh-and-bone bullies can make the leap to cyber cruelty with a simple click, post, or stream. Like a virus, digital bullies attack with a text, pic, or tag. They rain down the hurt from the cloud of pain in their life. Selfishly, they are trying to raise themselves up by putting others down with posts or texts about something hurtful, mean, or divisive, or something they think is "funny." To keep digital bullies from hating on your story, do your best to follow these digital life do's and don'ts:

1. Do be careful who you friend, follow, and like online.
2. Don't believe everything you find online.
3. Do a screen capture when a bully strikes and share the evidence with a trusted adult, like a parent, teacher, mentor, or school administrator.
4. Don't reply to offensive messages or retaliate.
5. Do be filled with integrity and always guard both your digital and analog life.

True OR False?

Life online isn't the same as real life, so digital bullying isn't the same as physical bullying.

False. Cyberbullying is real and very illegal. Online bullies can face arrest and prosecution because all 50 states have bullying laws that include harassment by electronic means that threatens another person's physical well-being.[5] The nationwide trend is toward greater accountability for bullying in general, both in school and off campus. Middle school students have been arrested for cyberbullying and charged with harassment, felony aggravated stalking, and even an offense against a computer system for unauthorized access, which is a felony.

DANCES

No less than two dozen recording artists have released songs titled "Dance Like Nobody's Watching." Not bad advice, if nobody's watching! The kids who take dance lessons growing up usually have a pretty easy time making it look simple on the dance floor. Those of us not so talented might find dancing around others a challenge. It doesn't matter if you have two left feet or own a pair of ballet pointe shoes, you should be able to have a great time at middle school dances. It's really all about hanging out with your friends and having fun. Don't sit around doing nothing! Get up, get down, cut loose, get in the groove, step to the beat, and dance like nobody's watching!

TRUE STORY

In the 8th grade I liked the coolest girl in school. She was smart, athletic, pretty, and always surrounded by popular guys with bigger muscles than mine. My only advantage was I owned a pair of parachute pants before any other guy in school. The pants were made of parachute-like material and featured multiple zippers on the legs for an extra edgy look.

I wore the parachute pants to the last dance of the school year. As the final song played, I took a chance and asked the cool girl to dance. She said yes. It was a slow song about a guy dancing cheek to cheek with a lady in red. And there we danced, like the song was written for us, I in my parachute pants and she in a red dress. I knew this was the start of something special. Suddenly the gym lights turned on, she ran over to her friends, I stood there alone, and the moment was lost. Later she signed my yearbook, "You're a really neat guy. See you next year!" Not a word about my parachute pants.

—JONATHAN CATHERMAN

DATING

The day is near when you'll want to spend some special time with a special someone you think is kind of special. *Ah, how embarrassing! Do we really need to talk about this?!* Actually, yes. Also known as dating, the act of spending time together to learn if you like them and if they like you is totally worth talking about. Now that you are middle school minded, think about this. What is dating? What isn't dating?

Let's start with what dating isn't. Acting silly to get attention isn't dating. That's called flirting. Staring from across the cafeteria isn't dating. That's called creepy. Going out of your way to walk by their locker between every class, following them home, and sending text messages that took you an hour to thumb peck isn't dating. That's called stalking. Don't be a creepy stalker. Dating is when both of you agree that you are going to get to know each other better, slowly. Seriously, there is no need to rush into things socially, emotionally, or physically. Socially, you don't need to make a big announcement to all your friends, in person or online. Emotionally, if you are going to use the "L" word, choose "like" and not "love" till you are way past middle school. Physically, only go as far as you would if your parents were watching. This may all sound weird, and if it does, don't worry, your future self will thank you.

True OR False?

Dates and figs are the same thing.

False. Figs and dates are two different types of fruits. Fig plants are shrubs, while dates are grown on trees.

DESKS

Front row or back corner? Beside the window for direct sun or close to the door for a quick exit? By yourself for better concentration or by your friends for more conversations? There are so many choices for where you can sit in class, you might not be able to stand yourself! But before your head gets lost in the cloud of options, keep your feet on the ground and this in your mind: One teacher may give you free-range pickings for where to rest your rear, yet in your next class the teacher could assign your behind to a seating chart. One thing is certain—all desks are "public property." The class before you and the one following have other kids sitting in the same seat. So respect the desk and keep the row straight, the circle curved, or the group together. Always try to leave your desk as good as, if not better than, the way you found it.

> On the first day of school, you got to be real careful where you sit. You walk into the classroom and just plunk your stuff down on any old desk and the next thing you know the teacher is saying, "I hope you all like where you're sitting, because these are your permanent seats."
>
> —GREG HEFFLEY (Jeff Kinney, *Diary of a Wimpy Kid*)[6]

DETENTION

It seems like everybody gets in trouble at school at least once. Trouble can range from something little, like forgetting to turn in homework and getting a bad grade on an assignment, to something serious that earns the discipline of detention. Google "meaning of detention," and the quick search results include the definition "the action of detaining someone . . . in official custody, especially as a political prisoner." Now STOP! Before you go and turn into a middle school student-rights activist, hold up and think for a minute. Consider that in the definition of the word *discipline* there is both the positive value of *knowledge* and negative action of *punishment*. Both are options. When you possess the positive value of self-discipline, you are more likely to do the right thing and not get disciplined with detention. Lack self-discipline, do the wrong thing, get in trouble, and be disciplined with detention. Basically you can have discipline and no detention or no discipline and get detention. The choice is yours. If you do find yourself *detained in official custody*, remember this wise advice from a seasoned 8th grader: Figure out what works and do it as often as you can. Figure out what doesn't work and stop doing it. That should keep you from getting in trouble more than once.

POP QUIZ

Q: What do ISS and OSS mean?

A: ISS stands for in-school suspension. This means you stay at school, do some work around the school, and get your schoolwork done. OSS is out-of-school suspension. You can't come back to school till they say it's okay, and getting your schoolwork done is much more difficult without the help of teachers.

DRAMA

Have you ever been in a situation where things got blown out of proportion and out of control really fast? All of a sudden something that wasn't that big of a deal becomes the biggest deal on the planet! Anytime an over-the-top emotional roller coaster is made out of the simplest of situations, it's DRAMA. And I don't mean the kind of drama performed on a stage. Yet, it's called drama for a reason. We are all characters in our own story, and when exaggeration is injected and judgments get emotional, your story becomes a drama. WARNING! Exit stage left when excessive drama is detected. Usually the situation is full of half-truths and a few lies. Don't get pulled onstage for the tragedy. Stick to what is positive and keep in control of your thoughts, words, and actions. Life contains enough real drama of its own, so there is no need to produce more.

In middle school, being onstage with my friends in theater class was a lot of fun. Any drama that happened off the stage was never good. Being kind and supportive to each other was always the best of times!

—ERICA CATHERMAN

LOOKING BACK

DRINKS

Thirsty much? Hope so, considering 60% of your body weight is water. Getting the wet stuff in is good for carrying nutrients to your cells and flushing out toxins from your body systems. Staying hydrated also helps keep your breath fresh and skin from getting too oily. A good goal is to drink about eight 8-ounce glasses of fluid a day. Everyone's body is dependent on fluids, yet few kids drink as much water as they need. Some even say they don't like the naturally tasteless flavor of water and prefer sipping down their fluids from an overpriced can of chemically sweetened carbonated water. Your preference for pure H_2O or H_2OCO_3 mixed with natural and artificial flavors is between you and your dentist. What you need to know about drinking water or soda at school is teachers, coaches, janitors, lunch assistants, bus drivers, and carpool parents all hate it when you spill. They're also not big fans of students leaving half-full drinks sitting around for somebody else to pick up or "accidentally" kick over. It's a good idea to check with your teacher/coach/driver about their beverage policy before you open a can of Get in Trouble at School.

LOOKING BACK

I'm really glad I got my own reusable water bottle. I filled it each morning with ice and water to drink at school. If I needed to refill it at school, I'd pick my favorite drinking fountain and top it off. Once I got home I'd fill it up again. I recommend a 24-ounce bottle that is dishwasher safe.

—REED C.

Just Joking

What is the study of soda carbonation?

Fizzics

ELECTIVE CLASSES

Some classes you are required to take. Some classes you choose to take. Many of the core courses like math, language arts, science, and history are required learning. Elective classes like drama, robotics, band, and computer programming are open for your choosing. The trick is being proactive and thinking ahead while planning your school schedule to include both your required and elective classes. The good news is, most of the class scheduling process is decided for you each year. Yet within your schedule are one or two class openings where you can "Insert elective course here." But choose wisely, because once you have committed to an elective class, it can be difficult to near impossible to change your schedule. So if Underwater Basket Weaving sounded cool when you signed up for it, but now Advanced Robotics is looking way better . . . it's probably too late. Don't forget to bring your scuba mask to class.

TO DO IN MIDDLE SCHOOL:

☑ Go on a class trip.
Most grade levels plan a class trip at least once a year. It may be somewhere local, historical, or just for fun. Sometimes a class trip may even be an overnight adventure. Whatever the trip, be sure to get the most out of the opportunity. Have fun, learn some cool stuff, and try to make a new friend along the way.

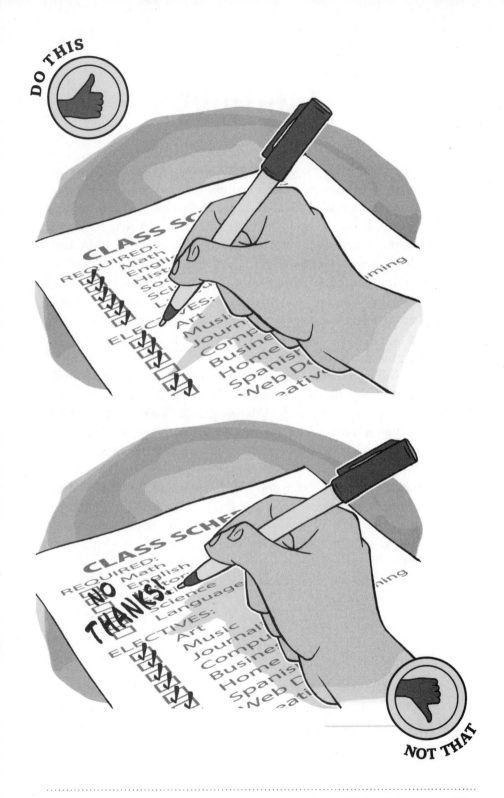

EMOTIONS

Ever ridden a roller coaster? All those ups and downs, twists and turns, spins and death-defying drops can make you feel nervous, scared, and excited all at the same time. That's a lot like the emotional roller coaster known as middle school. One moment you're feeling up, and then down. One day it's "the best of your life" and the next "the worst ever!" Why so many emotional twists and turns? Because middle school is life's prime time for no two days to be the same socially, emotionally, or physically. This can push you toward feelings of excitement and terror all wrapped up in one. But don't worry, it's pretty normal and will eventually smooth out in a turn or two if you do your part to stay on track.

For instance, when your emotions drop, it's not a good time to fly off the rails and experiment with cursing your way through "expressing" yourself. Nobody likes a dirty mouth. Choose your descriptive words carefully and try to stick with "I" language, like "I feel frustrated right now." Stay away from the emotional whiplash that follows blaming others for how you feel, with statements like "You are so frustrating!" They'll probably get defensive and say something back, like "No I'm not. You are!" and there you go again—up and down, round and round on the vomit comet of emotional twists and turns. Instead, go for a smoother ride by sticking with "I" language and avoiding the roller-coaster run of "you" language. When your emotions do get crazy, and they will, take a minute to chill out and remember that you are in control of you. Take a few deep breaths, stay centered, and focus on the positive.

POP QUIZ

Q: Which is the best emoji face to use when breaking up with someone in a text message?

A: Trick question! Don't break up in a text message. Face-to-face is the way to go unless that's not an option.

FACE WASH

Let's just face the facts. Those zombie apocalypse shows you're addicted to watching will never actually happen, yet a real-life zit invasion is headed your way. Stop obsessing over fictitious herds of bad skin–covered corpses and start planning how to defend your face from a puberty-planned pimple occupation. When it comes to fighting the effects of oily skin and acne, your best defense is a good offense. Start your day by washing your face in the shower. Wash again before going to bed each night. Always use a clean washcloth, mild face soap, and warm water.

HOW TO . . .

Wash Your Face

STEP 1—Make it routine. Wash every day, morning and evening.

STEP 2—Wet a clean washcloth with warm water.

STEP 3—Hold the warm washcloth to your face and neck for a minute. This loosens dirt and opens your pores.

STEP 4—Apply the mild soap to your face and neck. A nonirritating and alcohol-free skin product works best. (You can buy this kind of skin cleanser at most grocery stores or pharmacies. Ask your parent or a store clerk for help picking one that will work for you.)

STEP 5—Rinse your skin. Use warm water.

STEP 6—Don't touch! Your hands are covered in bacteria, and bacteria love to make zits on your face.

STEP 7—Eat and drink healthy. Avoid greasy foods high in saturated fat, sugar, and salt. Drink lots of water.

FARTING

There's no nice way to say it. Giving your backside outbursts cute nicknames like *tooting* or *a one-cheek squeak* doesn't change the fact that you just farted. Basically, we are all a walking science experiment that could blow up at any moment. Everywhere you go in school, a strange brew of noxious gasses ferments within you. Those bubbles building in your large intestine are produced "naturally" as your digestive system breaks down breakfast or lunch. The bloated feeling in your belly is nitrogen, hydrogen, carbon dioxide, and methane, which are all odorless gasses. If you are lucky, they might creep out undetected by the average nose. But mix in even a small amount of hydrogen sulfide or ammonia and your roux smells like . . . PEW! Was that you? Not if you pass on passing gas in class. Do the right thing and keep the shared air clean until you are outside. But when the pressure builds within and you just can't hold it in any longer, please let it out in the bathroom.

Just Joking

When a royal farts, is it a noble gas?

(That joke was for you science lovers.)

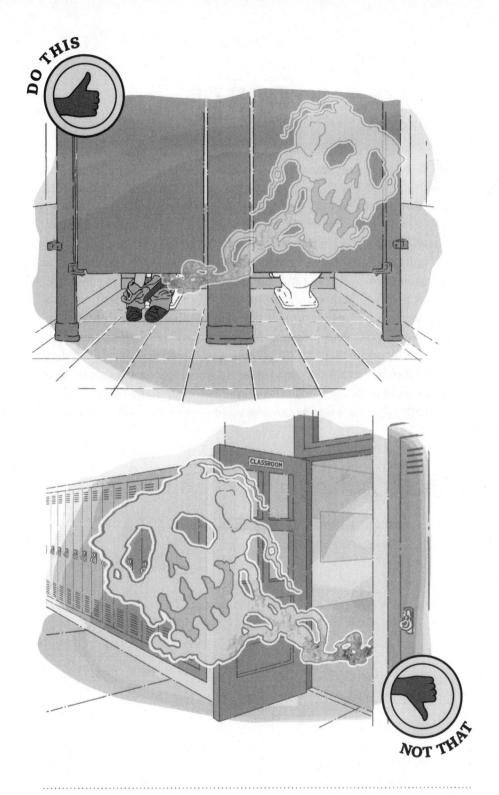

FIGHTS

It's like some kids are looking for a fight. Maybe they are selfish bullies, angry at life, or their cell phone just fell in the toilet. Whatever the reason for their thin skin and rush to "fighting words," there is no need to meet them in a punching, kicking, clothes-tearing brawl in the hall. Instead, show you are tough enough by being the one in total control. Be quick to listen, slow to speak, slow to become angry, and the first to use your brain by turning and walking away. Instead of raising their fists, smart people fight their battles with their brains. Not only is this a clever way to win, it also avoids the pain that comes with a potential bloody nose, bruised ego, and suspension trip to the principal's office. So the next time you feel like clenching your fists, remember that physical fights don't show true power or heroism. Unless you are in a boxing ring, the only fighting you should be doing is with the words you use to stand up for yourself and others who are unable to stand up for themselves. *That* is heroic.

Just Joking

Why don't skeletons fight each other?

They don't have the guts.

FIRE DRILLS

You know the drill. When wall-mounted sirens screech loud enough to make your ears want to bleed and mini strobe lights burn blue spots into your retinas, it's a fire drill. The school is not actually about to burst into flames . . . yet if a Bunsen burner had tipped over in science class and ignited the sweater you left dangerously close to an open flame, everybody would know how to get out of the building quickly and safely. But that's not the case today, so all you need to do is remember what you practiced back in the days of elementary school evacuations. Simply follow the teacher's instructions to make your way to the nearest fire-free zone. After a quick head count and the "all clear" is announced, you'll head back to class.

Do know that this is not the time to move slow, check your phone, or make a quick stop in the bathroom. Such behavior is not very bright and is guaranteed to make smoke blast out of your principal's ears while burning any chance you have of getting back on your science teacher's good side. Your best bet is to stay cool, calm, and cooperative through the entire drill. That, and remember to move your sweater off the counter when you get back to class.

POP QUIZ

Q: What three things are needed to make fire burn?

    (A) match, candle, paper

    (B) fuel, oxygen, heat

    (C) trees, marshmallow, tent

A: (B) fuel, oxygen, heat

FOOD

Health class teachers are guaranteed to say some funny stuff like, "You are what you eat, from your head down to your feet." Good thing this is not literally true. If such a statement were factual, some kids would look like a box of processed food parts soaked in an over-caffeinated carbonated beverage. Yet, what goes in must come out, and this happens in both obvious and obnoxious ways. The kind of food you eat has a direct effect on the quality of your life. The meals you choose power your daily energy levels, brain focus, the freshness of your breath, the smell of your gas, and even the number of pimples present on your face. Basically, food is fuel. Do your best to eat fresh and healthy, avoid junk snacks, drink lots of water, and limit your allowance of processed foods you choose to chew.

TO DO IN MIDDLE SCHOOL:

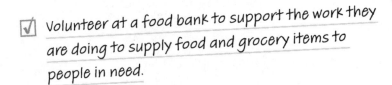 ☑ Volunteer at a food bank to support the work they are doing to supply food and grocery items to people in need.

FOOT ODOR

Okay, daydream about this for a minute. Imagine you are the first human to meet a tiny space alien whose ship crashed in your backyard. The extraterrestrial is peaceful and obviously really smart, because their head is huge (for a tiny alien). The little green thing likes you so much, our government makes you the alien's teacher about Earth's human stuff and a spy about space's alien stuff. All is good until your lessons about Earthlings include how our noses run and feet smell. In an attempt to help the confused alien understand the difference between runny noses and smelly feet, you offer the foreigner your shoe and a tissue. With only one sniff of your sneaker, the mini-Martian's skin turns from a light green to a puke gray. It gasps for air, its nose implodes, and then it chokes to death. To make a bad situation even worse, you learn the tiny alien is the royal child of the tiny alien monarchy with even bigger heads. This means you just killed the next in line to an alien kingdom with your rank, stank toe jam. The alien royals believe you just assassinated one of their own. They declare war on the third rock from the sun and prepare to hyper jump their Dreadnought Warships into a battle with Earth. Who knew your foul foot funk could bring about the end of the world!

Well . . . just about every human being has smelled stinky feet and knows the feeling of total doom. So how can you fight off an imaginary alien invasion and avoid the real-life embarrassment of walking around school with smelly feet? Start with washing your feet with soap . . . EVERY DAY! Next, dry your toes before putting on clean socks. Finally, air out your shoes at the end of the day and buy a pair of odor-eating insoles if you need to. These simple actions can save both your reputation at school and the earth from total annihilation.

STRANGE but True

Did you know that each of your feet contains a whopping 250,000 sweat glands and can produce a full pint of sweat per day, per foot? That's a lot of shoe-dew.

FRAGRANCE

Call it what you like—perfume, cologne, or simply fragrance—the act of adding scent to your skin has a long history. You could say the art of applying the air-altering aroma has been lingering around for thousands of years. The world's first recorded chemist was a perfume maker named Tapputi. Her methods for distilling flowers, oils, calamus, Cyperus, myrrh, and balsam date back to 1200 BC. But Tapputi's infusions were not the first fragrances to float through the air. Early mixologists throughout the Mediterranean, Mesopotamia, India, and Asia all experimented with fragrant scents to both sweeten the air and mask the foul smells. The fragrances we wear today include what many call *cologne*, or *perfume*, named from a Latin word that literally means "through smoke." It's important to apply it properly, in small amounts. Never are you to splash or spray a smoldering, thick, *through smoke* cloud of the fragrance on yourself, your clothes, or anybody else. The scent you choose has not been mixed to mask your BO, advertise your arrival, or loiter in the air long after you walk by. Wear it sparingly, and only occasionally, if you wear it at all.

HOW TO . . .
Apply Fragrance

STEP 1—Pick one scent. Don't mix scented body wash, deodorant, and hair products in the same air as your perfume, cologne, or fragrance.

STEP 2—Remove cap. Point away from your eyes when doing so.

STEP 3—Apply. Spray or dab a light amount to the skin on the base of your neck or wrist. Never apply directly to fabric, as the smell will change and can permanently stain your clothes.

STEP 4—Re-cap. You don't want to deal with a spill.

FRIENDS

Everybody needs a few true friends. Some say the number of truly great friends a person will have in their life can be counted on one hand. This is because there's a big difference between friends who will be there for you through thick and thin and virtual "friends" you collect after an attention-grabbing social media post. Your crew, squad, and besties truly know you and you know them. The best of friends are the ones who make you laugh, inspire you to think about new things, challenge you to do cool stuff, and are always there to lift you up. They encourage you to succeed, and when you do, they won't take advantage of you or the situation. Choose your friends carefully because you will be known by the ones you keep. This may mean you'll need to walk away from "friends" who are a bad influence. Most important, always be the kind of friend you'd like others to be to you.

> Find a group of people who challenge and inspire you, and spend a lot of time with them, and it will change your life.
>
> —AMY POEHLER[7]

GAMING

Reality is for losers who don't play video games—unless you are playing in virtual reality, and then you won't believe how lifelike the graphics have become," says the gamer totally disconnected from reality. Don't be that kid. Sure, gaming can be a fun part of middle school and beyond. So is being a professional in the RPG of life. Discovering the cheat codes to first-person interactions with family, teachers, friends, and other humanoids employs "reusable" hacks that work over and over again, just like in your favorite free-roam or sandbox game. To keep your real-world FPS rate smooth, commit the time and attention needed to master the game of life just as you would with the latest and greatest digital download. For sure the realities awaiting you outside the game are just as challenging and way more immediate than your cred as a galaxy-protecting mutant mercenary.

True OR False?

The first video game was invented in 1971.

False. Physicist William Higinbotham created the first video game in October 1958. It was a very simple tennis game, similar to the classic 1970s video game *Pong*, and it was quite a hit at a Brookhaven National Laboratory open house.

GET TO CLASS ON TIME

Getting to class on time is not as difficult as you may think. To prove the point, consider the following challenge. Emma and Nick are in the same history class. The bell rings and they leave for their next class at the same time. Their goal is to beat the bell and get there in five minutes or less.

- Emma knows what she's doing. She first stops at her locker. Then she walks over to say hi to a friend. Next, she makes a quick run to the bathroom, a stop at the trash can, and then straight to her next class. Total time 4:15.
- Nick chooses his own route. First, he goes to the bathroom, then to his locker. After stashing his gym shoes in the locker, he heads outside into the courtyard to yell "hi" to his friends. He rushes back inside and wanders the full length of the hall and back again. He drops his backpack on the floor and tries to jump over a trash can. Epic fail. Garbage and Nick spill everywhere. Acting like it never happened, Nick forgets where he dropped his backpack and searches the hall to find it. He grabs his backpack and stops to get a drink of water just as the bell rings. Finally, he runs around the corner toward his next class. Total time 5:57. He's late . . . also known as tardy.

The moral of the story? To get to class on time—be like Emma, not Nick. Sorry, Nick.

STRANGE but True

Some teachers will count you tardy if you are not in class by the time the bell rings. Other teachers will count you tardy if you are not sitting at your desk by the time the bell rings. It's your responsibility to learn what each teacher means by "tardy."

SCHOOL MAP

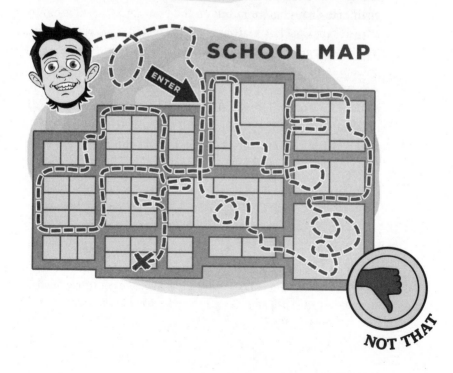

SCHOOL MAP

GOSSIP

The average human mouth can open wide enough to fit three fingers in between the upper and lower front teeth. That is, unless the words spilling from your mouth are gossip vomit, and then an entire foot may easily slip into the same space. "Foot in mouth" . . . what? It's just a saying, yet the meaning is time-tested. You see, way back in the 1870s, foot-and-mouth disease was all the rage with cattle. This was a problem and usually meant the cow was foul. The expression "putting one's foot in one's mouth" began to be used as a metaphor for foul people who got in trouble for what they said. Sharing selfish secrets, half-truths, and hurtful gossip got them in trouble then just as it does today.

Here are a few rules you can use to avoid putting your foot in your mouth:

Rule #1—If you have a problem with somebody, try talking with them rather than about them.

Rule #2—Ask yourself: Would you say to someone's face what you are wanting to say or post about them?

Rule #3—Talk about others the way you want them to talk about you.

If somebody is spreading gossipy stuff about you, refer back to Rule #1 and ask a trusted adult to go with you to talk with them.

> Anyone who will gossip to you, will gossip about you.
> —ANONYMOUS

GRADES

Trending news: Teachers don't "give" grades to students. Instead, students must "earn" their grades. Seriously, you've got to wrap your head around this one. In middle school you must do your part to pick up what the teacher is laying down. It doesn't matter whether or not you like the subject or teacher. Maybe you don't like the teacher's "style." Maybe you don't like the kids in your class. Do or don't, welcome to the big show. Middle school is all about you owning the effort you put into school to get the grades you need to succeed. For some kids, school comes easy. They still have to own their goal of getting straight A's in every class. Other students will have a more difficult time in school. They too must do everything in their power to make a grade that passes them through their courses. Here are a few sure-to-work ways to start owning earning your grades:

1. Come to class, on time.
2. Listen to the teacher.
3. Get organized.
4. Take notes.
5. Ask questions.
6. Don't distract other students or the teacher.
7. Be kind to the teacher.
8. Be kind to the substitute teacher.
9. Do the work and TURN IT IN.
10. Do any and all extra-credit work.

HOW TO . . .

Get Maximum Credit on Completed Classwork

STEP 1—Put your name on the top of the page.
STEP 2—Turn it in on time.

GRAMMAR

Not long ago, High English was the way people who wanted to sound smart talked. Slang-free and always proper, they spoke and wrote in a formal style that showed they knew the language of the educated class. Times have changed and so has the way people write and speak. In the world of a modern middle schooler, texting, DMing, and typing that is automatically spell-checked, autofilled, abbreviated, and filled with emojis is NBD. Similarly, the way some people speak has come to include verbal fuzz, mumbling, abbreviations, and slang that may or may not be understood by a teacher, coach, parent, and other students. Said simply, poor grammar can lead to a wealth of confusion. Avoid the confusion and show people just how smart you are by practicing two simple rules of good grammar.

> **Rule #1**—Speak up. You have a wonderful voice, so speak with the clear confidence needed for people to hear and understand you.
>
> **Rule #2**—Write well. BTW, teachers don't accept DM abbreviations in sentences, so spell out every word, using every letter.

When you speak and write well, people are more likely to understand, recognize, and respect you as a member of today's educated class.

POP QUIZ

Q: 1. What is the shortest sentence in the English language?

2. More English words begin with this letter than any other letter of the alphabet.

3. What is the longest English word that can be spelled without repeating any letters?

A: 1. "I am." 2. The letter s 3. uncopyrightable

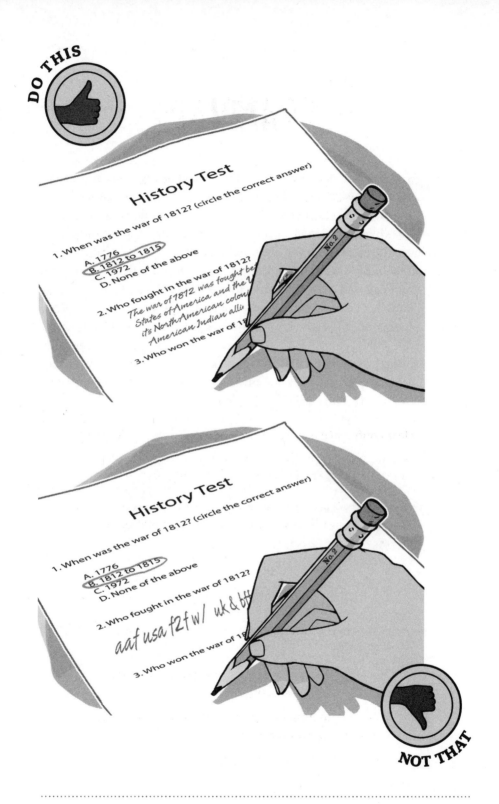

HAIR

Middle school is filled with unexpected challenges and more than a few frustrations. Finding a hairstyle that works shouldn't add stress to your life. Yet for some kids it does. Either they don't care that their head looks like a dirty mop, or they spend more time than an Instagram influencer directing each and every follicle into spray-held, sculpted perfection. You don't need to be either of those people. Instead, work your style until you find a 'do that works for you. Don't be afraid to try a few different looks before deciding on what looks best on your head. Next, find a barber or stylist who knows how to cut your hair the way you like, and stick with them. After that, use quality hair products to keep your style looking good. And please, for the sake of the noses surrounding you in class, never, never, ever apply fragrance-scented hair gels, pastes, sprays, or other trendy-smelling goo to your 'do.

STRANGE but True

Hair is strong. A single strand could hold 100 grams or 3 ounces in weight, but combined, the hair of a whole head could support 12 tons, or the weight of two elephants.[8]

HALL PASS

To travel freely over borders and between countries in the world requires you to carry a valid passport. To freely move around the school when you should be in class requires an official hall pass. Those are guarded like government-issued official travel documents. Most teachers don't just hand them out to anybody who asks. You'll need to pass two hall-pass application requirements. First, do you really need to go from here to there? Getting called out of class to visit the office, advisor, or media center or to deliver something from one teacher to another is approved hall-pass travel. "Needing" to get another drink of water, checking your locker, or faking a request to see the school nurse just as the math test starts are all unapproved travel requests and will be denied. Second, do you respect the power of the pass? Your reputation for past hallpass behavior can make or break your future pass privileges. The hall pass permits you the privilege to quickly go from point A to point B and back again. Hall passes are not a get-out-of-class pass, releasing you to free-range wander around the school. Respect the pass and all it permits you.

 Ask a Middle School Survivor

Q: When can I get a hall pass?

A: Hall passes are privileges. Getting a pass to try and hang out with your friends isn't a good idea. They should be used to go to the bathroom or get some water. If you abuse the privilege, you won't get a pass again.

—ANNA B.

HALLWAYS

Hallways are the highways of school. Routes exist to move the middle school masses and their cargo from one school stop to the next. Like downtown traffic during rush hour, your school hallways will occasionally get all jammed up bumper-to-bumper and even report a few shoe flat-tires and fender-bender backpack accidents. To keep traffic moving and the hall cops off your tail, follow these basic road rules to arrive at your next destination on time. Always walk on the right side, yield to teachers, look both ways when turning toward the lockers—and no parking in the middle of the hall! People stop being polite when a "few friends" stand in the middle of the flow "just talking." Like a dam, they back everything up, and frustrations grow deep, fast. When they do break free, it's a slow rush to beat the bell through the very mess they created.

HOW TO . . .
Pick Up Your Papers When Dropped in the Hallway

STEP 1—Stop, drop, and protect your papers. They are about to get trampled. Don't just stand there and look confused.

STEP 2—Scoop up the dropped papers. Don't worry about keeping them in order.

STEP 3—Stand back up and keep moving. Hold on to your papers tight so you don't drop them again.

STEP 4—Step aside and try to organize the mess of papers you hold. If something is missing, go back and attempt a recovery mission.

HANDWASHING

Think about all the stuff you touch at school. Your two hands grip doorknobs, handrails, seats, lockers, desks, hall walls, gym floors, and countless other sticky surfaces. Then with filthy fingers you dig around in your bag for a sharp pencil. One minute later you stick that putrid pencil in your mouth. Without thinking about it, you just chewed on a yellow #2 stick of germs, bacteria, and microscopic viruses. One way to combat self-contamination is to wash your hands a few times a day at school. For sure wash them after every visit to the bathroom, before lunch, and after science class, gym class, and trips through the locker room. Wash for at least 20 seconds (enough time to sing the "Happy Birthday" song twice). Think you can handle it?

STRANGE but True

"A large percentage of foodborne disease outbreaks are spread by contaminated hands. Appropriate hand washing practices can reduce the risk of foodborne illness and other infections."

—Centers for Disease Control and Prevention[9]

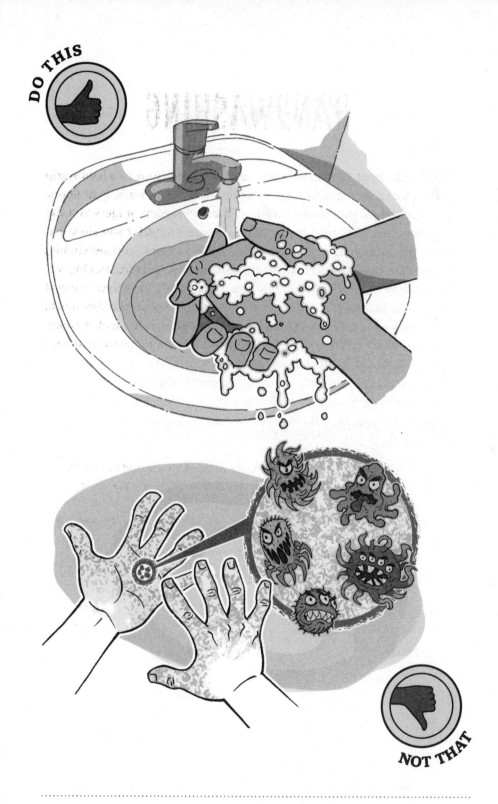

HANDWRITING

The ancient Egyptians wrote in hard-to-read scripts called *hiero-glyphs*. To read and understand their writings requires the keen eye of a trained professional. Well, you're no young pharaoh, and your mummy may still need to help you with your English homework, so leave the archaeologists in the sand and let's work on your handwriting. For the last six years you have practiced your writing skills, which means you should be pretty good at it by now. Capitalizing letters at the beginning of each sentence, crossing your t's, dotting your i's, and fitting each word between the lines on the paper is exactly what teachers expect of all middle school students. If you still insist on wandering all over the page with your words, scratching out letters that you don't even recognize, and ending sentences with odd punctuation marks, then move to the desert and chisel your hieroglyphs into the walls of a pyramid. No? Well then, slow your scroll, keep it between the lines, and always remember your penmanship.

What did the paper say to the pencil?

Write on.

HOME ROOM

It's been said that a kid's room is their castle. You know who lives in castles? Royalty. You know who lives in the castle's dark and dirty dungeon? Lazy jokers. Don't be the lazy joker who claims it's regal to carpet their room with dirty clothes, molding food, and "lost" homework. Instead, be the ruler of your kingdom and govern your room with a decree to keep the space clean enough for a royal.

STRANGE but True

Having a clean room or space has been linked to self-control and making better choices in regard to food and delaying gratification for a better outcome. Messy rooms or spaces have been linked to creativity . . . and higher allergies and illness due to higher levels of dust, dead skin cells, molds, and bacteria.[10]

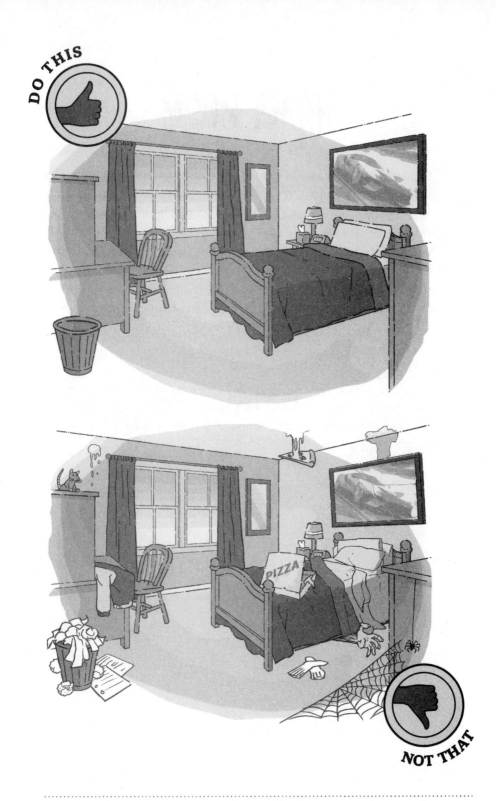

HOMEROOM

The plan for homeroom is to start the school day off right. Often homeroom time is used for teachers to take attendance, share some announcements, and get ready for the day ahead. Yet some students feel their homeroom at school is an extension of their room at home. These kids figure if they were home, they would be sleeping, so why not catch some z's at school too? Well, rise and shine! Think of the school bell that starts homeroom as your second alarm clock, without the snooze option. The sun is up, you are awake, and the school day is ready to go.

TO DO IN MIDDLE SCHOOL:

 Join a club or sport.

HOMEWORK

Some teachers are all about assigning homework **and some are not.** Some class subjects require you to read, study, **write, or prepare** outside of assigned time in school. There is no predicting **how often or** how much homework middle school will require, **but one thing is for** certain—it's best to get it done and handed in . . . **on time. The crazy but** true part is that teachers often see students "forget" to hand in **finished** homework more often than they see them actually **forget to finish their** homework. That's like going out to dinner, ordering, **and paying for the** food . . . but forgetting to eat it. Once you get it done, hand it in . . . **on** time. Oh, and one more thing. Make sure to put your **name on your** homework before you get it done and handed in . . . **on time.**

Just Joking

What did the calculator say to the math student?

You can count on me.

LEADERSHIP

Do you want to be a leader? Good. You will need to be more influential than you are easily influenced. If you are influential, then you can be a leader. An easy-to-remember definition of *leadership* is "Leadership is influence, used for good." Middle school is the prime time to dream, discover, and develop your levels of influence to benefit both yourself and others. First, you'll need to practice self-leadership. Begin with taking responsibility for your own actions and doing what's right, even when nobody is watching. Work hard to get better at what you enjoy and practice the life skills and moral character that will help you move from where you are to where you need to go. Add in some time-management skills and you'll be the leader of you. Second, look for opportunities to lead others. Leading others requires you to treat them as you would want to be treated, listen well, and value teamwork. When others see these values in you, they will want to follow and learn from you. That's when it happens. By using your influence for good, you'll have become a leader.

> Do not wait for leaders; do it alone, person to person. Be faithful in small things because it is in them that your strength lies.
>
> —MOTHER TERESA

LOCKDOWNS

As you know, every school must perform lockdown drills. "Lockdown. Lockdown. Lockdown." Not much has changed since you practiced lockdowns in elementary school, so you know what to do and what not to do. There is no need to make it into something it's not or to draw attention to yourself. Instead, do the right thing and keep calm, follow instructions, stay hidden, remain still, be quiet, and don't mess around. The school receives a grade on how well the drill goes, and the higher the grade, the better.

 Ask a Middle School Survivor

Q: Are lockdowns the same in middle school as they were in elementary?

A: Really, lockdowns are the same in all schools. If you have experienced a lockdown in elementary school, it's the same in middle and high school. The rules are all the same. Nobody gets in the building and nobody gets out.

—BRENDA L.

LOCKER LOCKS

Middle school may be your first experience with lockers. Love them or not, lockers provide a safe place to store your things so you don't have to carry around extra stuff from class to class. Remembering to lock your locker is a really good idea. Forgetting how to unlock your locker is a really bad feeling.

Mind-blanking your locker combination is often followed by a feeling of panic and an audible "AAAAHHHHHHHH!" Other symptoms of locker-combo memory block include sweaty palms, shortness of breath, blurred vision, shaky hands, dry mouth, stomach pain, and the false feeling of world-ending panic. In an effort to avoid such exaggerated symptoms, follow this two-step procedure:

STEP 1—Memorize your locker combination and practice cracking the code as many times as you need to never forget it. Seriously, drill those numbers so deep into your brain you'll still remember them the day you graduate from high school.

STEP 2—Repeat step 1 until you get it right, every time.

HOW TO . . .

Open a Standard Combination Lock

Turn #1—Spin right (clockwise) three full turns. Stop at your FIRST number.

Turn #2—Spin left (counterclockwise) one full turn, passing the FIRST number, and stop at the SECOND number.

Turn #3—Spin right (clockwise) and stop at the THIRD number.

Pull open lock.

LOCKER ROOMS

Hopefully, the dreaded days of stinky locker rooms are a thing of the past. No longer forced to shower after exercise, we now use the locker room as a place to quickly change before and after gym. Good thing, too, as a little sweat in your gym clothes can go a long, smelly way if you leave them on the rest of the day. So it's best to change into something fresh before returning to class. Although showers are out, making sure you have a clean shirt to change into and a fresh swipe of deodorant is a good idea. Take care to keep your bag and clothes off the floor, as it's a petri dish of germs, mold, and fungus down there. For the same reason, you need to stay off the tiles too. Sit on the benches and chairs, or stand if you must. Just NO SITTING on the floor! Also, just like you do following a visit to the bathroom, always wash your hands after using the locker room. Though you don't take showers at school, make sure that you get one at home. Consider hygiene your homework and shower each and every day . . . it keeps the stinky bacteria away!

 Ask a Middle School Survivor

Q: Why do we need to change clothes in a locker room?

A: Because you need to change into your gym clothes somewhere, and changing in a bathroom stall is not an option. Stashing your school clothes and stuff in a gym bag or locker is a good way to keep your things safe. Just get in, get changed, and get out again. Nobody is watching and nobody cares. Just be sure to wear clean underwear.

—REED C.

LOCKERS

Some students really love their lockers. They decorate, theme, and create a DIY space worth showing off. Others treat a school locker like their future first cheap apartment—a cramped, dark, smelly place just big enough to stash a few things. Either way, most lockers tend to transform over the course of a school year as the space begins to collect snack wrappers, dirty gym shirts, trash paper, and a few "missing" class assignments. Basically, if you need to call in a search party to locate a library book in your locker's rubble, you've got a problem. But you can avoid the mess by keeping your locker nice and neat. Maintain love for your locker by keeping it free of trash, unneeded papers, and for sure those smelly gym clothes—take them home and wash them. This will keep your locker a welcome stop all year long. Pictures and flashing string lights are optional!

 Ask a Middle School Survivor

Q: How many times a day will I get to go to my locker?

A: It depends on your school and the rules they have. If you have "free" passing time, meaning you can go where you want during your passing time before your next class, then you can go to your locker when you want. Sometimes, instead of going to your locker after/before every class, it helps to bring stuff for two or three classes so you don't have to go to your locker so much.

—EMILY R.

LOST AND FOUND

So, you have cleaned out your locker but still have an item missing. Chances are good it's been collected and is now in the middle school lost and found—a great place to find "lost" items you didn't mean to leave behind in class, in the gym, or on the bus. It's pretty funny to see what items go missing. Here's a short list of real things students have lost and found in middle school.

Found

cowboy hat, straw	eyeglasses, prescription
lunch bag, Marvel	hammock
mini Statue of Liberty	beach ball, multicolor
math binder, algebra	retainer case, with retainer
snow pants, blue	dog collar, no dog
fishing pole, no line	plastic globe, coin inside
black glove, left hand	flashlight, no batteries
headphones, red	tree ornament, Christmas
diary, unlocked	tablet, green case
backpack, green	shoe, right

"Found—shoe, right" . . . Really?! Who loses one of two shoes and doesn't notice? How did that student walk home from school, thinking, "Something feels different. I don't know exactly what, just different"? Really? Look down. You're missing a shoe! If you find yourself claiming the title of The One-Shoed Wonder or just can't find your jacket, lunch bag, glove, or mini Statue of Liberty, take the time to stop by the school's lost and found. You may have to dig through the collection of unclaimed treasures for your missing jewel. Just remember, "finders keepers" only applies if it really is yours. There's no "shopping" for five-finger discounts in the lost and found.

Just Joking

What do you call a bear that lost its teeth?

A gummy bear

LUNCH

Everyone's heard an adult say, "Don't talk with your mouth full. It's rude." If you can't remember ever hearing such table instructions, you were polite from birth or you forgot—again. Lunchtime is a balance between talking with your friends and eating your midday meal. Your body needs the fuel while your friends need to talk about the latest episode of your favorite post or YouTube video. The good news is you can do both, just not at the same time. The rule is simple. Say it, don't spray it. Eat a few bites. Chew and swallow. Talk for a minute. Take a drink. Swallow. Take another bite. While chewing with your mouth closed, be a good listener to what your friends are saying. Swallow. Talk again. Repeat. Lunch is also a good time to work on making new friends. Try a new table, be inclusive, ask someone who is sitting alone to join your table. Who knows? You could make a new friend or make someone's day!

True OR False?

Eating with your mouth open is considered polite in some cultures.

True. In some cultures, slurping while drinking and chewing with your mouth open show the cook or host that you find the food delicious, while in other cultures such behavior would be considered extremely offensive. So be sure to study up before you chow down.

LUNCH LINE

Next in line. Next in line, please. What do you want for lunch today, sweetie? Fruit with that? A cookie too? How about some milk or juice with your meal? Next in line, please. Next in line."

Making your way through the school lunch line is a lot like selecting a meal at your local fast-food restaurant. True, there are fewer choices, no soda, and you can't mega-size a school lunch—but you're still supposed to move fast through the food line. Just like ordering at McJacks or Taco King, it's best to know your options before it's your turn. Waiting to decide until after the lunch person is staring at you is too late. Make your choice, fill your tray, and don't forget a drink. Finally, don't rush, and no pushing as you head into the lunchroom to find your friends.

HOW TO . . .

Pack Your Own Lunch

STEP 1—Select leftovers from the refrigerator or make a fresh sandwich.

STEP 2—Pick a healthy balance of food that includes a main item, a fruit or vegetable, and a treat. Don't forget a bottle of water.

STEP 3—Put each food item into a sealed bag or approved food container.

STEP 4—Pack all your lunch items in a lunch bag or box. Add an ice pack if you've got perishables, like meat or dairy or mayo.

LYING

Good thing the childish taunt "Liar, liar, pants on fire" is far from factual. If it were a statement of the obvious, how often would smoke trail up from behind you following a fib? One thing is for certain: When you lie, you're going to get burned. Teachers, principals, coaches, and even bus drivers are really good at turning up the heat when they know your story lacks honesty. Chances are, they have heard the same tall tale told before and recognize your false testimony for what it really is. A lie. So face the facts and be truthful. Honestly, it's much cooler.

Just Joking

Never trust the periodic table.

It makes up everything.

MEDIA CENTER/LIBRARY

See those rectangular-shaped things on the shelf? Those are called books. They are like TV for smart people. The media center has them stacked all over the place. Those machines on the tables are computers. Like books, they too can open doors to discovery, lead to great adventures, and be your ticket to more information than any one person could consume in their lifetime. Or the media center may seem like slow, quiet torture for the middle school student who thinks they already know all they need to succeed. Why read when there's a video? Why study when Google and AI know all the answers? Why, why, why? Well, because only a fool hates wisdom and learning. And you're no fool. So enjoy a little quiet time. Crack the cover of a book and use a computer for more than videos. You never know what you'll discover.

TO DO IN MIDDLE SCHOOL:

☑ Find and visit with a couple of your favorite teachers from grades past. Thank them for all they taught you and share your current successes with them.

MONEY

Money is like magic. With a simple distraction and sleight of hand, it can disappear into thin air. Now you see it. *Poof!* Now you don't. And what do you have left? An empty soda can, a crumpled bag, and a bad case of what feels like indigestion but is really buyer's remorse from getting what you didn't need and now don't want. The trick to managing money in middle school is figuring out how cash works more like a tool and less like candy. "Yeah, but I like candy," is what you're thinking—and you're right, who doesn't?

The truth is, the older you get, the bigger and more expensive the things you buy get. So now is the time to master your money and stop believing the illusion that your money grows as you do. The truth is, you are running out of teeth to put under your pillow, the few bucks your grandparents slip into a birthday card only come around once a year, and your parents are not an open bank vault. What money you can make from pet sitting, babysitting, or doing extra work around the house can be put to work for you. Here's how. Save in the bank as much as you can, spend as little as you must, and give to charity as if you were the one in need. This makes you the master of your money and keeps you from being mastered by money's many sweet illusions.

> The art is not in making money, but in keeping it.
> —PROVERB

NAIL TRIMMING

According to the Guinness World Records, the person with the longest fingernails on a pair of hands is a woman from Minnesota, USA, named Diana Armstrong.[11] Measuring over 42 feet, 10 inches, the combined length of her 10 fingernails is longer than a standard yellow school bus! Not so great while texting, but you can bet she could scratch every inch of her back. Don't be the long-nailed version of Diana at your school. Keep your fingernails trimmed, and whatever you do, NO biting!

STRANGE but True

Lots of germs and some nasty bacteria live under your fingernails. What kind, you ask? The kind that hang on after making a trip to the bathroom, touching your shoes, or petting a dog. Think about that fun fact next time you nibble on your nails.

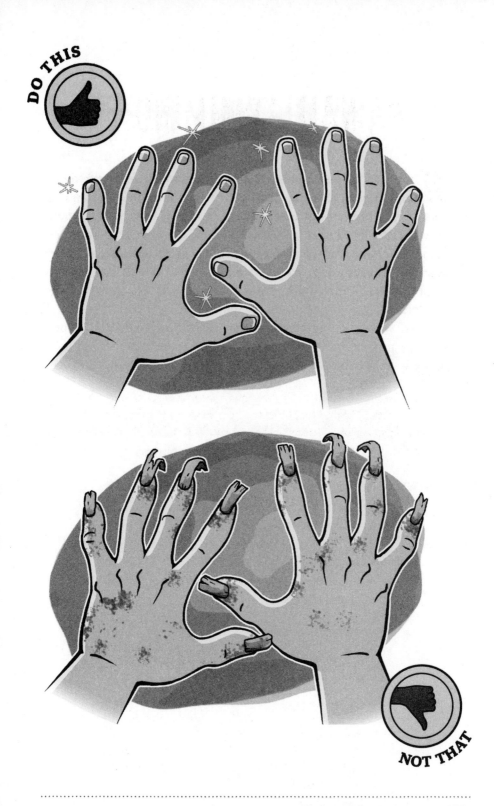

NAME ON YOUR PAPER

You did all that homework. You studied, researched, and worked hard to write what feels like an A-grade paper. You stuffed it into your backpack, went to school, and even remembered to turn it in on time. A few days later the teacher hands back the graded assignments and yours is "missing." She points you to a stack of papers on her desk, and there you discover your work. Graded down from a B+ to C+. What the what? Then you see it. Across the top of the page is written, "No name." What?! You forgot to put your name on the top of the page. Seriously? After all that hard work, you forgot the simplest part of the assignment? The only part you are guaranteed to get right? Come on, now! Name it and claim it. Always remember to put your name on the paper before handing it in.

HOW TO . . .
Remember Somebody's Name

STEP 1—Introduce yourself. Tell them your name and ask theirs.

STEP 2—Repeat their name in your head and in a sentence. Like this: "You said your name is Shawn? Nice to meet you, Shawn."

STEP 3—Try to associate them with somebody else you know with the same name.

STEP 4—Use their name whenever you talk with them. This will burn their name into your memory.

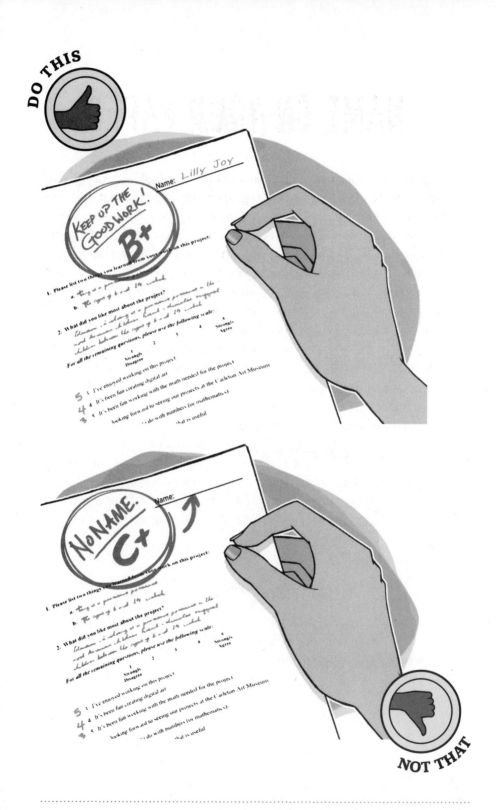

ONLINE

But I found it on the internet, so it has to be true." Um . . . no. Just because you read something online does not make it true. The truth is, back in 1983, researchers began assembling a computer-based "network of networks" to share data between universities and government organizations around the globe. This early version of what would become the internet wasn't very cool until 1990 when a British computer scientist named Tim BernersLee, also known as TimBL, invented the World Wide Web. From then to now, the interweb has spun from telephone landline dial-up to wireless go-anywhere connectivity. People used to "go online" occasionally. Today you live much of your life online. From googling "who is TimBL" to the GPS location tracker on your phone, you are leaving digital footprints, fingerprints, and imprints everywhere you virtually and actually go. This can make your life easier or bring it crashing back to reality. Keep your posts pure and you'll be cool with your teachers, parents, future college applications, and job interviews. Remember, it's important that you never share personal information about yourself online! Go rogue while connected and you'll have some explaining to do about what your eyes have seen, thumbs have clicked, and where you were online when that spyware accidentally infected your device.

STRANGE but True

The first website went live way back in 1991. It is dedicated to information about the World Wide Web and is still active today. You can check it out for yourself at http://info.cern.ch/hypertext/WWW/TheProject.html.

PARENTS

Chances are, when your parents were in middle school, reusable water bottles, smartphones, social media, and trending videos weren't a big thing. Their idea of password protection was a secret phrase whispered in a friend's ear before entering a play fort or cushion castle. A lot has changed since your parents were in middle school, so you'll have to give them a break every now and then when they just don't understand. Really, parenting is no easy task. Few other adventures in life can bring more joy or pain to a person than the responsibility and privilege of parenting. You'll want to add to the privilege they have of raising you by scoring some positive points with the parental units as often as possible. Here are two of the best ways: Spend time with them and talk to them. Time spent together and talking about stuff, or through stuff, is how good relationships are built. The better your relationship, the happier both you and your parents will be. They may not know what it's like to be in middle school today, but you can teach them. They may or may not agree with all you share, but you'll be amazed how smart they become by the time you're a parent and your kids are in middle school.

> A father's goodness is higher than the mountain, a mother's goodness deeper than the sea.
>
> —JAPANESE PROVERB

PDA

It's only appropriate to get a little technical here. PDA is the abbreviation for *public display of affection*. No duh, right? But have you ever really thought about how odd middle school PDA can be?

Public: (adjective) open to all persons
Display: (verb) to show or exhibit; make visible; flaunt
Affection: (noun) fond attachment, devotion, or love

Basically, PDA is putting the physical side of a "relationship" on show for all to see. There are varying degrees of PDA. On the body-contact Richter scale, "0" equals nobody ever sees you two together and "10" equals everybody knows everything. A PDA hug registers in at about "2." We're not even going to discuss holding hands, kissing, or other stuff, as most schools discourage that kind of physical affection anywhere on campus. And that's probably a good thing when we consider most relationships in middle school don't last very long. Like only "a couple of days to a few weeks" not long. Just because you are "going out" doesn't mean you need to be "making out" in the hall. Nobody wants, or needs, to see that. Dealing with math tests and forgotten locker combinations is tough enough.

Did You Know?

There's no such thing as "butterfly kisses." As kids we received fluttered eyelash "kisses" against our cheeks and were told they were butterfly kisses. The truth is, butterflies do not have any lips or teeth, just a long, coiled tongue. Gross.

PHYSICAL EDUCATION

Some students look forward to PE class as a welcome break from the rear-numbing task of holding down a desk chair. Other kids walk to gym class thinking, "I'm really more of the brainiac type." Well, guess what? Like it or not, exercise boosts the brain's power. People who move more than their mouth outperform seat surfers in simple tasks like long-term memory, reasoning, attention, and problem-solving.[12] It's true, look it up. That, and a healthy young person like yourself is capable of walking about 12 miles a day without feeling the pain. Unless you haven't moved that far in weeks, which means you're probably growing tired from just holding this book. Look at it this way: Physical education class is way more than running, jumping, and doing sports-like stuff a few times a week. Exercising your body builds your muscle strength, physical coordination, and brain-processing power. Put all those benefits together, and it's good to know that if the zombie apocalypse ever does come, you'll be able to both outthink and outrun the walking dead.

 Ask a Middle School Survivor

Q: **What should I know about changing from gym clothes back into my school clothes?**

A: Changing shorts and a T-shirt is no big deal. Just remember to take your gym clothes home each day to wash them and ALWAYS have deodorant to apply during the school day.

—CAROLINE L.

POP QUIZZES

Okay, everybody. Please put your books away, sharpen a pencil, and prepare to take an unscheduled test.

Question #1—What is the secret to passing pop quizzes in middle school?

"No, no, don't tell me. I know this one."

The answer is _____ (*Fill in the blank*)

Or would you prefer to try your luck with multiple-choice answers?
   (A) I studied for this all week.
   (B) I looked at the chapter practice questions last night for three minutes.
   (C) I cheat off the answers of the kid sitting next to me.
   (D) All of the above.

Answer: (A) There is no need to question the fact that middle school is a virtual minefield of both expected and surprisingly too frequent "I didn't know we had a quiz today!" tests. From the weekly exam to pop quizzes that come out of nowhere, the only answer to passing tests in class and life is to study ahead and be prepared for the unexpected. Good luck.

Correction . . . good studying.

> **What kind of tree does a math teacher climb?**
> Geometry

PREPARED FOR CLASS

You beat the bell and made it to class on time. Now, are you prepared for class to start? Ask any teacher and they will agree the top 10 things you need to bring to class each day include the following:

1. Pencil (with eraser)
2. Pen (blue or black)
3. Lined paper (wide or college ruled, depending on the class)
4. Completed homework (finished before class starts)
5. Class textbook (when provided)
6. School-provided technology (charged and ready to go)
7. Calculator (a must for math and science)
8. Personal technology (if allowed)
9. Rested eyes (that means sleeping in your bed at night and not in class)
10. Self-motivation, confidence, drive, grit, humility, manners, and a willingness to learn (okay, that's seven unique traits, but just saying "character" wouldn't do)

True OR False?

It's the teacher's job to hand out pencils to whoever forgot one.

False.

PRINCIPAL

Who's the boss? You know, the big shot, big cheese, big wig, big kahuna? Kingpin, kingfish, King Kong? Top dog, top brass, guru, all-pro, CEO? Who's the brains around here? The principal is, of course. But why? What have they done to deserve the leader-of-leaders title? Well, most public-school principals have earned at least a master's if not a doctoral degree. That means they were in school as a student for somewhere between 17 and 19 years before getting the job. That doesn't even count the years of experience they had in the classroom as a teacher or in the front office as a vice principal. It's a pretty good bet that they've been around school longer than you've been alive. It's also pretty safe to say they chose to work in middle school because they like you. "But what's not to like?" you ask. Really? Middle school administration is not the easiest way to make a living. Your principal has to deal with a limitless flow of drama, crazy hormones, know-it-alls, and a daily dose of "What just happened here?" To make both your day and theirs the best it can be, try introducing yourself to the principal. Let them know you appreciate them and all they do for the school. Sound strange? Come on, this is middle school. You can do it. And don't worry. The principal may be the top dog around campus, but they don't bite.

True OR False?

Some principals are so committed to their job they sleep at the school.

True. A principal in Asotin, Washington, told his students that if they could raise $10,000 in the school fundraiser, he would sleep on the school roof overnight. Students raised $22,000 in pledges, and Principal Nicholas slept on the roof, in a tent, in a sleeping bag, in the middle of October.[13]

PROBLEM-SOLVING

One of the biggest differences between immature and mature middle school students is their ability to problem-solve. Immature students need their teachers, parents, and friends to solve all their problems. Mature students work to resolve their problems on their own the best way they know how. Immature people say stuff like, "I can't do the work because I don't have a pencil." Mature problem-solvers ask a friend for a pencil before the test begins. When two students fight over who gets to sit by the window during a science lab, they are immature. When they work together to move two chairs together on the window side of the lab table, they are mature. If "You didn't tell me what homework I missed when I was absent" has ever crossed your lips and assaulted a teacher's ears . . . yep, you guessed it. Immature. By asking the teacher, "I missed class yesterday and am wondering what homework was assigned," you demonstrate your maturity level and ability to problem-solve.

TRUE STORY

"Houston, we have a problem." In 1970 the manned space mission of Apollo 13 had a massive malfunction in their CO_2 filter system. The lives of three astronauts hung in the balance unless a solution could be found. Working together, a team of problem-solving men and women back on Earth found a way to fit a square filter into a round hole. Their proactive can-do efforts saved the Apollo crew and made for a great story, which was scripted into the blockbuster movie *Apollo 13*.

PUBERTY

As much as your school life is changing, so is your body. Thanks to puberty, a daily shower is a must. Soon your hair will grow out of your legs, underarms, and in places you guard like PRIVATE PROPERTY. Your body will start to mature into its adult form, and zits will become your sworn enemy. For some kids, puberty is scary at first, but it doesn't need to be. Even the hormone-driven mood swings can be managed by taking good care of yourself—eating right, exercising, staying hydrated, and getting enough sleep. The good news about puberty is that it's an important step in you growing up. Nobody stays forever young, except Peter Pan and plastic surgery–addicted celebrities who live in their own kind of make-believe. Middle school is no fairy tale, and puberty isn't the horror movie some make it out to be. What can you do to make the most of this awkward yet important stage of life? Don't fight it. Embrace the changes and take care of yourself. Just as caterpillars become butterflies, kids become adults. The transformation can feel confining and uncomfortable, but the end result is totally worth it.

POP QUIZ

Q: How old are most kids when they begin puberty?

A: First signs of puberty usually start between the ages of 8 and 13.

RAISING YOUR HAND

"Ooh, ooh, ooh, call on me. Call on me. I know it. I know this one. I know. Over here. Right here. Me, me, me. Call on MEEEE!!!!!!"

There you are, waving your arms around, hands raised high, and you know the teacher can hear you begging for a chance to be heard. But nooooo. They call on the kid sitting over there all calm, hand barely raised over their head. That, or the teacher calls on the kid who's not even raising their hand. What? Why? Well, let's see if you know the answer to this one, smarty-pants. Are you pushy? Do you ever blurt out the answer? Do you have an expert opinion for every question the teacher asks? Or let's consider the opposite. Do you hide in the back of class and avoid all contact with the teacher? When you are asked a question, do you shrug it off and mumble, "I dunno . . ."?

Let's go with this. It's a good idea to raise your hand from time to time when you know the answer. But it's never good to be a know-it-all all the time. Kids who try to sit all quiet, hoping not to be noticed, will eventually be asked to speak up. Chances are, the one time the teacher does volunteer you to share is the exact time you don't know what the teacher is talking about. Your best plan is to raise your hand with an answer when you know the answer, at least once a day. It's not hard. Simply lift your hand over your head and make eye contact with the teacher. When they call on you, share what you know or ask a good question to help you learn more. It's also good to raise your hand to ask good questions every now and then. If you don't get what the teacher is teaching, put that hand up and ask a question. Ask good questions and you will get good answers. Ask shallow questions and you can expect shallow answers. Ask no questions and you will get no answers.

HOW TO . . .

Fake an Answer

STEP 1—Trick question! Your teacher already knows the answer to the question they just asked. Do you really think they are new to this? Seriously, they are a credentialed pro and you're just trying to fake it. Nice try.

READING FOR FUN

Those who read can go anywhere, do anything, and be anyone they choose. Readers transport through time from ancient days to futuristic fantasies. Readers have seen the glory of a hero's adventure and the intrigue of true mystery. Readers have looked out over a sea of adoring fans chanting their name and stood alone against the wrath of an enemy determined to destroy. Readers fly on the backs of dragons and explore the depths of space. Readers are the first to discover and the last to abandon their imagination. Kids who read can travel the world, save the universe—or multiverse—and live a thousand lives before finishing middle school. People who never read will live only once.

> **"**A book is like a garden, carried in the pocket.**"**
>
> —CHINESE PROVERB

> **"**Not all readers are leaders, but all leaders are readers.**"**
>
> —HARRY TRUMAN, the 33rd president
> of the United States (1945–1953)[14]

READING FOR SCHOOL

Okay, here's the situation. Your homework this weekend is to read chapters 8 and 9 for your world history class. On Monday morning there will be a closed-notes test worth 10% of your final grade. What will you do? If you're thinking it's a good plan to read the chapters and take notes about the important parts, then you are setting yourself up for success come test time. If you are thinking reading is dumb and taking notes is a waste of time because there are no important parts, um . . . good luck with that. A good plan is to finish the assigned reading before the assigned time. How you do this is up to you, but do plan your reading and work your plan. Some kids like to just "get it done" all at once. Others prefer to read for a few minutes here, a few minutes there, and then push through with an hour of no interruptions and good note-taking. Try a few strategies until you find the one that helps the reading stick with you. Remember, just pushing through the words does you no good if you can't recall what they said. You never know, you might just read something new and cool enough to remember after the test.

 Ask a Middle School Survivor

Q: What happens when I don't do the summer reading the middle school assigns?

A: The school will mark it down as a bad grade. I really don't think you want to start the year off in trouble. Summer reading is one of the first grades of the year, so you'll want to do your very best.

—MACY S.

REPORT CARDS

Report cards are a lot like sports scores. How a team performs on the field or court shows up on the scoreboard without bias. That means no coach, official, or fan can just toss up or take off points to make a team look better or worse than they actually performed. The same is true about your report card. Teachers can't just "give" you a good or bad grade. What they post in report cards is an accounting of how you performed in their class. Basically, you did the work and they kept the score. If you want to keep score too, you can. In fact, a good game plan includes you knowing how well you are doing in each class day to day. Most middle schools give you access to an online grading system where you and your parents can see which assignments are handed in, which are missing, the grades you've earned, test scores, and extra-credit points. You'll be able to see, track, and predict what your score/grade will be on report card day. This way you can own your own grades and not just wait for the end of the game to learn the score.

TO DO IN MIDDLE SCHOOL:

 Make A-B honor roll.

RESPECT UPPER GRADE LEVELS

Fear and respect are two different things. You have no need to fear the students in the grades above you. Yet, showing them respect is a must. The best advice is simply to treat your "elders" like you would want to be treated. Show them some respect by being polite and staying cool when they are around, and they are more likely to be good to you too.

STRANGE but True

In Tibet, sticking out your tongue is a greeting and a sign of respect. But to the Māori people of New Zealand, sticking out your tongue is part of the war chant preceding battle.

SCHOOL PICTURES

Look at the camera and smile. This is for the yearbook, not a mug shot. Posing for a school picture is nothing new to you. You've been doing it since you were in kindergarten. The difference now is that the picture captured in middle school will not just get sent out to grandparents to be posted online, framed, or hung on their fridge—that pic is also going into the yearbook. Come the end of the school year, that book will hold you forever captive between the two kids with last names alphabetically beside yours. So what is your plan for picture day? Besides wearing an outfit that is both cool and clean, keep these do's and don'ts in mind as you strike your pose.

1. Do smile
2. Don't make a weird face in hopes it will go viral
3. Do tilt your head slightly
4. Don't overtilt your head
5. Do try to look natural
6. Don't try to look like nature

Really, it's up to you. It's not like people are going to keep that school picture forever. Oh wait, yes they will. Say cheese.

LOOKING BACK

When your mom tells you what to wear on school picture day or to pull your hair back so she can see your face, it just proves she still cares. Truth is, you'll wear what you want. But don't forget, that's the pic everybody will see in the yearbook.

—ERICA M.

SHAVING FACE

Before you head into the halls of middle school, I mustache you a question. Have you taken a good look at your face in a mirror lately? See anything growing on your upper lip? If not, you might soon. Now is about the time some guys see the peach fuzz just below their nose start to turn darker, grow longer, and begin to look like lip moss. Patches of odd-length beardness will soon grow on their cheeks, and catlike whiskers may randomly sprout out of their chin. When this happens, don't freak out. They are not turning into a yeti, just yet. Instead it's time to consider learning how to shave. Until then, don't worry if your mug is free from facial follicles. It won't be long before scraping overpriced precision-cut steel blades across your tender skin will become a daily test of your blood-letting avoidance skills. You can read some sound how-to instructions on shaving your face in Jonathan's book *The Manual to Manhood*.

" I like shaving with a dull razor. **"**

—SAID NO MAN EVER

SHAVING LEGS

Look at your legs. Yes. Is the hair growing on your walkabouts beginning to grow longer and thicker? If so, it may be time to consider shaving. In some parts of the world, shaving may be optional, and today some women in the US let their leg and armpit hair grow free. But if joining the pro–body hair movement isn't for you, you'll need to take the time to start shaving. To help you avoid razor burn, nicks, or cuts, you can read specific how-to instructions on shaving in our book *The Girls' Guide to Conquering Life*.

TRUE STORY

I shaved my legs for the first time when I was in 5th grade. I borrowed my mom's razor without asking and mowed down my leg hair. A few minutes later my legs were minus hair and plus a few razor-burn bumps and one bloody nick. When I showed my mom what I had done, she wasn't very happy. Mom cried and said I was too young. Looking back, I should have asked my mom for help. I probably could have avoided the razor burn and blood, but my mom would probably still have cried.

—ERICA CATHERMAN

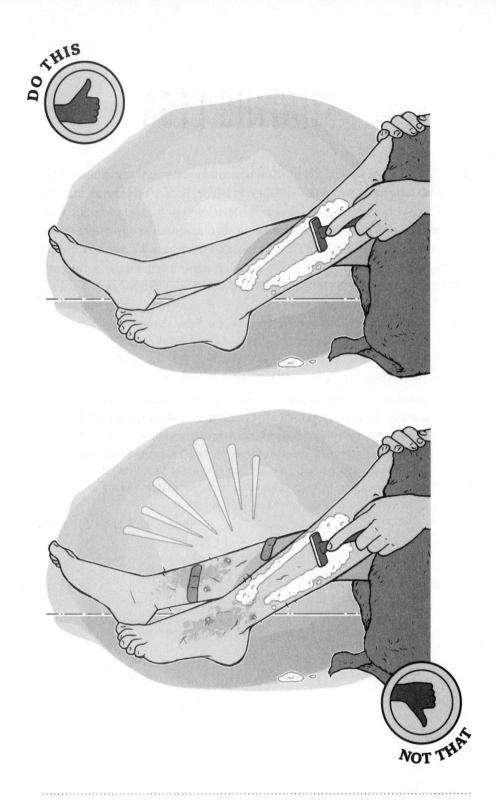

SHOWERING

You know what really stinks about middle school? Some of the middle schoolers. *FLASH!* That's the bright light of truth flipping all the switches on. Now maybe it will be easier to see that what might look clean doesn't always smell clean. And that includes the bodies of middle school students. But wait. There's more to smell in this story, and it's not all roses. Think about it. By the time a parent, teacher, friend, random weirdo, or pack of mean kids says they can smell your personal blend of BO, how many other people noticed too? Only one person was brave, or socially insensitive, enough to say something. So what can you do to avoid the embarrassment of being IDed as the stinky one? Here's a good plan. It's time to start showering. Every day! Yes, you read right. Every-single-stinking-day! One of the facts of life is that showering daily is part of growing up. An unwashed middle school body can quickly become encased in a dingy and often smelly layer of dirt, sweat, and tweenage hormones. Soap, shampoo, water, and a clean towel are the only real way to refresh your natural self and keep people from turning their noses away when you walk their way.

POP QUIZ

Q: Why does using soap when washing work?

    (A) Magic.

    (B) Soap allows insoluble particles to become soluble in water so they can then be rinsed away.

    (C) Because my mom says so.

    (D) Both A and C.

A: (B) Soap allows insoluble particles to become soluble in water so they can then be rinsed away.

SIBLINGS

Older, younger, twins, half, or step, the classification of relation and age range between you and your sibling(s) matters little. The fact is, by the time you are in middle school, you'll have spent about 33% of your spare time with your siblings. That means you have hung out with your stinking brother or nosy sister more than with your friends, teachers, parents, or even by yourself.[15] The quality of the time you spend together probably ranges from hugs to thugs. One minute you are best friends, the next mortal enemies, and then back to good by dinner. You share looks and a last name, a branch on the family tree, and maybe even a room in the house. The most important thing about dealing with your siblings is learning that as you grow older, they aren't going to be important people in your life—they'll be some of the *most important* people in your life.

True OR False?

Some twins can be the same and the opposite at the same time.

True. Some twins are literally mirror images of each other. This means they have the same physical features but on opposite sides of their body. If one twin is righthanded, the other is left. Some mirror twins can even have mirror organs. One's heart is on the left and their twin's heart is on the right. Even their skeletal features can be reversed.[16]

SICK DAYS

Sick or not sick? That is the question. If you are, stay home. Nobody at school needs to be exposed to your clammy hands and prepuke face. If you're not really feeling bad, don't lick your palms or whine about fake symptoms in an attempt to avoid some test you "don't feel good" about taking. Believe it or not, you have a limited number of sick days before passing a class or grade level becomes a real headache. When you do miss school for a day or two after yacking into the porcelain throne, be sure to have a parent's or doctor's note for the office with an explanation of your absence. And to all you actors out there, keep this fun fact in mind: Once you've faked sick a few times, nothing short of barfing up a lung will convince people you really do need bed rest.

TRUE STORY

The Kissing Disease

The 8th grade was the best two years of my middle school life. Seriously, I repeated the 8th grade because I'd been absent for two months, sick with mononucleosis. This energy-draining illness is also known by the shortened title "mono" and its nickname favored by my friends, "the kissing disease." I liked my buddies' nonclinical diagnosis the best because it cast me as the one and only guy in our group of friends who had any puckering experience. (She would have been a sick girl, but a girl with willing lips nonetheless.) The problem was, I had no idea how I acquired the illness. My lips had no kissing history, and in fact they would not for another year, at least.

—JONATHAN CATHERMAN

SKIPPING SCHOOL

What's the big deal? It's not like skipping school is illegal or anything. Well, actually . . . it is. Skipping school is legally called *truancy*, and truancy is illegal for middle school students. Decide not to come to school and you'll rack up an unexcused absence. Unexcused absences add up to makeups, including detention, Saturday school, summer school, and even fines issued to your parents. "Yeah, but school takes up so much time and I never really learn anything anyway," you say. Okay, smart kid, let's do the math and see what you know.

There are 365 days in a year, totaling 8,760 hours. The average student goes to school for about 6.5 hours a day, 180 days a year. That totals out to about 1,170 hours per year in school. On average you'll sleep 7 hours a day,[17] totaling 2,555 hours a year. Nine hours a day will be connected to media,[18] ticking up to around 3,285 digital hours per year. You'll spend about 30 minutes a day in the bathroom, flushing away 182 hours a year. Now, if you've been keeping track, that leaves you with about 1,568 hours per year to do whatever you do in addition to going to school. So let's be honest here. With all those media minutes you probably spent multitasking while doing other things, you really have more "free time" than expected. It's basic math. Skipping school is illegal and doesn't add up to be a very valuable way to spend your time. Then again, smart kids like you who go to school know this because you've learned how to do the math.

Just Joking

Grandparent: "Keep your voice down! The caller ID says it's your school. Must be because I let you skip today!"

Grandchild: "Please don't answer. I told them I was attending your funeral!"

SOCIAL MEDIA

*M*uch Ado About Nothing is a play penned by William Shakespeare way back in the late 1500s. It's still popular today with middle school English teachers, so you may be reading it soon. The word *ado* means trouble or difficulty, and that's what the play is all about. Much of the ado in the play comes from a few handwritten letters that cause confusion, gossip, and misdeeds to spread quickly. If Shakespeare were writing the play today, he might exchange those handwritten letters with modern-day social media posts. Seems realistic, considering most people's social media is much *to-do* about nothing and can easily cause much *ado* about nothing. Think of the time we spend paying attention to what took somebody next to no time to post. Here's a simple Shakespeare-approved line worth memorizing. It may just keep you out of much ado in future social media posts: "Not everyone needs to know everything about you."

True OR False?

Internet addiction disorder (IAD) affects up to 8.2% of the population in the US and Europe.

True. Many teenagers use social media and believe it's an important part of their lives. Yet some can get addicted to social media, causing their virtual life to negatively affect their real-world relationships and responsibilities. As powerful as alcohol and drug addiction is, IAD includes social media addiction as a real thing, which may require professional intervention.[19]

SPORTS

In middle school you'll have your first opportunity to play on a school sports team. Some of the kids who show up for tryouts may have played in rec leagues for years, while others are giving the game their first shot. There is no guarantee the athlete with more experience will make the team. Coaches are looking for team members who want to play, are teachable, and are willing to work hard to get better. Sure, raw talent is good, but ask any seasoned pro and they'll tell you exactly what it takes to win: "Hard work beats talent when talent doesn't work hard."[20] So get out there and run, jump, shoot, hit, throw, flip, spike, and sweat your guts out. Make the team, and you can expect to win some games and lose some. What matters most in sports is not the ranking of your team, size of the trophies, or who scores the most points. What matters most is how you play the game as a TEAM. Together Everyone Achieves More. Also, you have a good time!

POP QUIZ

Q: When were the first Olympic Games held on the plains of Olympia?

(A) 1910

(B) 1896

(C) 776 BC

A: (C) 776 BC. "The first ancient Olympic Games can be traced back to 776 BC. They were dedicated to the Olympian gods and were staged on the ancient plains of Olympia. They continued for nearly 12 centuries until Emperor Theodosius decreed in AD 393 that all such 'pagan cults' be banned."[21]

STEALING

Kid #1: "Finders keepers, losers weepers."

Kid #2: "Yeah, but you found those headphones inside my backpack."

Kid #1: "Don't try to confuse things with a technicality."

Isn't it interesting how "finders keepers" seems to always work in favor of the "finder"? Then when something of theirs gets "borrowed," they feel horribly wronged and believe the entire world is out to get them. Seriously? There are no five-finger discounts in middle school or beyond. Seeing something you want and just taking it is stealing. We have a law here on planet Earth that basically says, "Thou shalt not steal." Also known as theft, robbery, lifting, forced sharing, or borrowing without permission, stealing is stealing. But why do some kids feel so entitled to "claim" other people's stuff? Because they lack personal integrity. When a person has integrity, your stuff is safe around them because they too believe in doing the right thing, even when nobody's watching. Be that kid.

> Integrity is doing the right thing, even when no one is watching.
>
> —UNKNOWN

STUDYING

Today is Monday. The test is on Friday. When will you study? The right answer is "A little bit each day." The wrong answer is "Tomorrow." It's easy to find at least 50 excuses for why today is not a good day to study. You're busy, tired, hungry, bored, brain-dead, or rebelling against the system. Besides, you'll just cram the night before and ace that test on Friday. Fail. Here are a few study tips from a professional brain scientist who knows a thing or two about how the mind of a middle school student works. If you want to ace the test, try these study strategies on for size:

1. **Break it up**—Turn your study sessions into mini-lessons. Don't try to memorize the names of all the state capitals in one sitting. Instead, learn a few every day over a few days. Be sure to review what you learned last before starting the next set.[22]

2. **Move around**—Try studying the same stuff in a different place next time. You are more likely to remember the names of the state capitals when you move from studying in the library to your kitchen table, to the backyard, or to the gym after basketball practice. This forces your brain to form new associations with the same information, and that makes your memory sticky.[23]

3. **Work it out**—Getting some aerobic exercise builds more than your muscles. Research shows that running a couple laps around the house or doing a few jumping jacks between study questions will improve your brain-processing speed.[24]

True OR False?

By sleeping with a book under your pillow, the information will infiltrate your brain while you dream.

False. Dream on.

SUBSTITUTE TEACHERS

Students say lots of things about substitute teachers. Some of what they say is true. Most of it isn't.

"I hear we have Mr. Garvey as a substitute in math today. My friend's sister's locker partner was in band class with a kid who says Mr. Garvey is really nice and that he thinks homework should be illegal, so he never gives it. I'm going to love him."

"I hear we have Miss Smith as a substitute in PE today. My brother knows this kid who used to go to school here but moved last year, and he said Miss Smith used to be a Marine drill sergeant and gives kids detention if they can't do 50 push-ups. I hate her already."

"I hear we have Ms. Holly as a substitute in history today. I heard this 8th grader say twice that she shows kung fu movies in class and keeps the ashes of her dead dog in the back seat of her car. She is so weird."

Before you believe everything you hear about a substitute teacher, consider giving them the same break you'd want them to give you. Instead of being quick to judge, try getting to know them a little bit first. You may be surprised to learn most substitute teachers are pretty normal people doing a really tough job for not much pay.

Just Joking

Walking through the hallways of the middle school, a principal saw a new substitute teacher standing outside a classroom with their forehead resting against a locker.

The principal heard the substitute mutter, "How did you get yourself into this?"

Knowing they were assigned to a difficult class, the principal tried to offer the substitute some support. "Are you okay?" they asked. "How can I help you?"

The substitute teacher lifted their head and replied, "I'll be fine as soon as I can get this kid out of their locker."

SWEARING

There are 191 four-letter words in the English language that start with the letter *f*. Most are *fine*, yet a few are particularly *foul* and should *fail* to ever *flow from* the mouth hole in your *face*. In its simplest *form* you'll *find* cursing, swearing, profanity, blasphemy, and vulgarity all *flop flat* and *fall* to the lowest *form* of spoken expression. President Abraham Lincoln once said that it's "better to remain silent and be thought a *fool* than to speak out and remove all doubt."[25] Sure, dropping a *fury* of f-bombs in a *free-flow furl* of *foul flak* is *fuel* for *fake fame from fain fans*, but in *fact*, it's never clever. Verbally shocking *folk* with the *fail* of *foul* language is like playing in traffic. It's guaranteed to get people's attention *fast*, but in the end, the *fool* will *feel* the greatest pain.

Just Joking

Why did the chicken go to ISS?

Because it was caught using fowl language.

TEACHERS

Recent advancements in human research have uncovered a remarkable fact about student and teacher interactions. When exposed to powerful doses of the positively charged element Hu+, teachers often absorb the contagious properties of kindness in high concentrations. Hu+ then reproduces rapidly in the exposed subject and is released again by reverse osmosis toward students in close proximity. This amazing finding may sound impossible, yet in test after test the evidence is conclusive. Put simply, when a student is nice to a teacher, the teacher will be nice back to the student. You can test this method, often referred to as the Golden Rule experiment, for yourself on your teachers. Your findings could change the world as you know it.

TRUE STORY

Before he became the mega celebrity for his roles onstage and in movies like *X-Men*, Hugh Jackman was a school gym teacher. One of Mr. Jackman's former students was Rollo Ross, who grew up to become an entertainment reporter. As luck would have it, Rollo Ross got the opportunity to interview his former teacher at a red-carpet event. Just as Rollo started the interview, the teacher in Mr. Jackman came out. "Rollo, I'm sorry, mate," Mr. Jackman interrupted, "but we go way back. I used to teach you at a high school in PE, and I want to know how your physical education is progressing. It's very important to me." Mr. Jackman continued and totally surprised Rollo with a pop quiz when he asked, "How is your education going? Did I set you up for life?" Luckily for Rollo, the Wolverine was in a good mood and enjoyed joking around with his former student.[26]

TESTING

Tests are part of school—and life. You'll hear some middle school students say stuff like "I'm good at math, just not at taking tests." Okay, let's compare this test-taking trouble to life outside the classroom. Can a soccer team's starting striker be good at kicking the ball, just not during the game? Or what if a musician claimed to be a great rapper, just not when performing? You would never go to a doctor who knows all about healing people but forgets what to do during surgery. The trick to how pros perform under pressure is similar to how you can set yourself up for test-taking success. The professionals have performance strategies, and good students do too. A good strategy for doing your best on a test is to have a proven plan for your test prep, taking, and completion. Here's a tried-and-true plan for you.

Test Prep

Study well in advance of the test.
Get a good night's sleep before the test.
Eat a good breakfast and drink some water.

Test Taking

Listen to the teacher's instructions.
Read each question or passage all the way through before answering.
Answer the questions you know first.
When you don't know an answer, eliminate options you think are wrong.

Test Completion

Use any time you have left to double-check your work.
Make sure your name is on the test.

Do the math: $\begin{array}{r} 111111111 \\ \times\ 111111111 \end{array}$

Answer: 12345678987654321

TEXTING

On December 3, 1992, a 22-year-old test engineer named Neil sat at his computer and sent the first SMS text message to his friend Richard's phone. The message shared between the friends was a holiday greeting that read "Merry Christmas."[27] What started with one message in 1992 is now estimated to be 27 billion messages sent per day. That's over 18 million messages per minute. This means there's no escaping the short messages, and that can be a problem for you in middle school. Here's why. Splitting your attention between two or more tasks is called *multitasking*. Doing homework and texting is multitasking. Studying and texting is multitasking. Riding a bike and texting is multitasking. Walking and texting is multitasking. The problem is, our brains can't do either activity well when we try to do two tasks at once. When students try multitasking while doing schoolwork, they are splitting their attention. The quality of their learning gets really shallow. Students remember less and have trouble linking their learning to where it can be used in life. That, and we tend to run into things while texting and moving. Walking, riding, or driving and texting don't mix well. The same goes for texting and doing schoolwork. To get the most out of your reading, homework, and study time, you'll need to put the phone away. Your friends may wonder where you are for an hour, but your brain and body will thank you for a lifetime.

HOW TO . . .

Lose Your Cell Phone to a Teacher in 5 Steps or Less

STEP 1—Sneak a text message in class.

STEP 2—Act surprised when the teacher sees you.

STEP 3—Deny sending a text message.

STEP 4—Claim your freedom-of-speech rights are being violated.

STEP 5—Hand over your cell phone.

TRACK THE TEACHER

Tracking your teacher does not mean identifying their footprints and trailing them through the school's habitat and into the staff lounge. That's called *stalking*. Stalking is creepy and illegal. Stalking a teacher would probably get you suspended. Tracking your teacher is perfectly legal and helps keep you on the teacher's good list. To track your teacher, simply look at them when they are talking. If they move from one side of the class to the other, you keep watching them as they go. Hence, you track their progress through the lesson they are teaching.

STRANGE but True

People get paid to read body language. Experts in reading people's body language can make a living teaching their skills at seminars or working with police departments to determine by a suspect's body language whether they are lying.

TRASH

Somebody gets paid to pick this up." That's what some kids think when they leave their trash behind instead of tossing it away. They walk off, expecting somebody else to clean up after them like they employ a personal staff of merry maids. Seriously?! Technically, that's called *littering*. It's also called rude, selfish, and lazy, and it's a totally rotten thing to do. What if this was their house? More specifically, what if people left litter behind in your bedroom? Out of sight, out of mind, right? No way! You would strongly refuse (not be willing) to let other people's refuse (trash) pile up for you to pick up. The same rule applies at school. Toss your rubbish, and when it does fall short of the garbage/recycling can, own your litter recovery and leave no trash behind.

Just Joking

Why was the cafeteria trash can so sad?

He just got dumped.

VOICE CHANGES

Puberty kick-starts the growth of your body, and over the next few years, you'll go through a lot of dramatic physical developments. One of the most noticeable changes is one you won't see—you'll hear it. The change in the pitch and tone of your voice is a good thing. It happens when the vocal cords in your larynx, also known as your *voice box*, lengthen and get thicker. Think about it like this. Your vocal cords are like rubber bands. When stretched out and plucked, a thicker rubber band makes a different sound than a skinny one does. Puberty changes the thin vocal cords' bands in your larynx into thicker cords. Along the way, your voice may crack and squeak from time to time. Just consider each squawk as proof the puberty process is working. Don't worry and don't get embarrassed or mad. To help keep your voice in check while the transition is happening, try talking at a controlled volume level. This should help, yet there are no guarantees in puberty.

TRUE STORY

I was talking with a good friend at school when my voice went haywire. I said three words and each one sounded like it was broken in two pieces. My friend's face froze and their eyes got wide. We both thought, "What just happened?" My face turned red and we started cracking up, laughing. We didn't say anything about my voice; we just laughed. It was an awkward situation, but nobody really cared. Voice cracks are normal in middle school.

—COLE C.

VOICE VOLUME

Here's a quick vocal lesson for beginners. Sound is measured in units of frequency called *hertz* (Hz). The hertz of a woman's voice ranges between 165 and 255, while a man's words measure between 85 and 155 Hz. The result is, many women's voices sound higher than men's. No duh, right? But wait. Check out the vocal range of the typical kid entering middle school. The pre-puberty voices of both girls and guys wave in at 250 to 300 Hz! Add this high-pitched truth to the odd fact that kids' lung pressure is 50–60% higher than adults' and what do you get? The answer isn't quiet.

Yet there are ways you can make your voice sound more mature. First, when in large groups, quiet down. The combined audio adrenaline of a class talking all at once can be high-pitched enough to make dogs howl and stress a teacher out to the breaking point of assigning extra homework. Second, when you are called on in class, speak up. The class needs to hear your answer, and when you speak clearly and calmly, your voice is less likely to rise, peak, or sound flustered. In other words, your hertz will sound more mature.

True OR False?

The smallest bone in the human body is located in your ear.

True. The stapes is the smallest of three tiny bones in the middle ear that convey sound from the outer ear to the inner ear.

WRITING PAPERS

Handwritten or typed out, every good paper is drafted in steps.

STEP 1—Choose the topic. If the teacher assigns you the topic, then that step was easy.

STEP 2—Research information. This can be done online or in those ancient texts known as books. Either way, use only credible sources that are fact, not fan fiction.

STEP 3—Draft an outline. What are the general ideas you want to say in the beginning, middle, and end of your paper? How many points will you make along the way?

STEP 4—Organize your notes. You'll need information and notes on each of your main points.

STEP 5—Write a first draft. Don't worry about too much editing here. Just get your thoughts down in an organized way.

STEP 6—Edit the paper. Do your best to make sure what you are writing makes sense and flows well. Check for correct spelling and grammar.

STEP 7—Have somebody else edit the paper. Be open to suggestions and be willing to make any needed changes.

STEP 8—Prepare the final work. Format your paper exactly as the teacher assigned, and be sure to put your name on the top of the first page. Staple or bind the work as instructed and hand that thing in on time. Nice job.

POP QUIZ

Q: Which animal can run the fastest: an elephant, a squirrel, or a mouse?

A: An elephant. Elephants can run up to 25 miles per hour.

YEARBOOK

Captured forever on high-gloss paper, yearbooks are lasting proof of the best and many of the most embarrassing moments of middle school. Between the pictures of kids having fun, sports, clubs, and every student's portrait, your friends can sign and write their own thoughts. Here are a few of the least creative yet most common comments.

"Have a great summer." "Stay cool!" "Don't ever change." "Glad I got to know you." "Hope to see you next year." "Message me sometime."

Then there are the kids who put a little effort into what they write in their friends' yearbooks. Check out these original comments.

"If you like water, then you already like over 60% of me." "I love it when I start laughing and you start laughing at me so hard you gasp for breath. You should know most of the time I'm laughing it's because I just passed gas." "Any size pizza is a personal pizza, if you believe in yourself." "I waited 1,095 days to write this in your yearbook. Hi."

Write what you like; just remember people tend to keep yearbooks for the rest of their lives. Go ahead and get one, write in your friends', and feel free to laugh in the future at what everybody wrote about, gas or not.

TO DO IN MIDDLE SCHOOL:

☑ Buy a yearbook.

ZOMBIES

Believed to be reanimated corpses capable of moving about in herds or in solo pursuit of brains to consume, zombies are feared by apocalypse preppers worldwide. The truth is, such beings are purely science fiction, unless you count some middle school students. Just watch the door of the school prior to first bell. There you will see students streaming in with glazed looks on their faces, hair matted, legs dragging, and drool spilling from their mouths. They are zombies! Or are they? Perhaps a logical explanation for their mindless herdlike movements is a lack of sleep, poor nutrition, and the belief that the day holds no real value. So how do you combat such a virus?

The antidote to zombieness is not as rare as you may think. To protect yourself, follow this three-part zombie-vanquishing plan and spread the word to anyone who will listen. First, get 8+ hours of sleep every night. Second, eat a good breakfast every morning. Third, look for something new and cool to discover and develop in yourself every day. That's it. Zombies are not real, yet students who live nearly numb lives are. Think of it this way: If you're not learning, you're not living. So go make the best of everything, and be sure to fill your middle school brain with good stuff. This time of life only comes once, so make the most of each and every day.

LOOKING BACK

Middle school was full of ups and downs, kind of like a roller coaster. But roller coasters are fun, right? Whether or not you like roller coasters, embrace the changes middle school and puberty bring. In the words of my younger brother, "Do what YOU do and be who YOU be." Meaning you don't need to be like everyone else: The world needs YOU. Find confidence in who you are and what you do. Embrace your changes and allow yourself time to grow and mature. Be strong, kind, brave, humble, and courageously adventure on.

—ERICA CATHERMAN

RIDDLE ME THIS

1. A rooster sitting on the peak of a barn roof lays an egg. The peak of the barn roof faces north and south. It is the longest day of the year and the sun is directly overhead. Which way will the egg roll?

2. What do you fill with empty hands?

3. What goes around the world and stays in a corner?

4. What has one foot on the right, one on the left, and one in the middle?

5. What shows up once in a minute, twice in a moment, and never in a thousand years?

6. Two fathers and their two sons go shopping together. They each buy one bag to take home with them. They do not lose any bags, and yet when they arrive at home, they only have three bags. How can this be?

7. You're a bus driver. At the first stop four people get on. At the second stop eight people get on. At the third stop two people get off, and at the fourth stop everyone gets off. The question is, what color are the bus driver's eyes?

8. A sheriff rode into a small western town on Friday. The sheriff stayed two nights and left on Friday. How could that be?

9. What belongs to you but is used more by others?

1. Roosters don't lay eggs. 2. Gloves 3. A stamp 4. A yardstick 5. The letter *m* 6. There are just three people: a grandfather, his son, and his grandson. 7. The same as yours; you're the bus driver. 8. The sheriff's horse's name is Friday. 9. Your name

10. I'm light as a feather, yet the strongest person on Earth can't hold me for more than five minutes. What am I?

11. Can you name three consecutive days without using the words *Wednesday*, *Friday*, and *Sunday*?

12. What runs but never walks, often murmurs, never talks, has a bed but never sleeps, has a mouth but never eats?

13. They come out at night without being called and are lost in the day without being stolen. What are they?

14. The more of me you take, the more you leave behind. What am I?

15. What has a head and a tail but no legs?

16. What do you call a lemon that hits the floor?

17. What has six faces but doesn't wear makeup and also has 21 eyes but can't see?

18. What does a snow person like to eat for breakfast?

19. Why did the scarecrow win so many awards?

20. What did the glove say to the ball?

21. Where do TVs go on vacation?

22. You can see me in water, but I never get wet. What am I?

23. What has cities but no houses, lakes but no water, and forests but no trees?

24. I have keys but no locks. I have space but no room. You can enter but can't go outside. What am I?

10. Breath 11. Yesterday, today, and tomorrow 12. A river 13. Stars 14. Footsteps 15. A penny 16. A lemon drop 17. A die (dice) 18. Frosted Flakes 19. They were "out standing" in her field! 20. "Catch you later." 21. Faraway, remote places 22. A reflection 23. A map 24. A keyboard

25. It's been around for millions of years, but it's no more than a month old. What is it?

26. What building has the most stories?

27. I am the only organ that named myself. What am I?

28. What kind of coat can only be put on wet?

29. Anthony's mom has four children. Her first child is a girl named April. Her second child is a girl named May. Her third child is also a girl and her name is June. What is the name of her fourth child?

30. Forward I am heavy. Backward I am not. What am I?

31. What has hands but no feet, a face but no eyes, and tells but does not talk?

32. I never was. I am always to be. No one has ever seen me, nor ever will. Yet, all expect me. What am I?

33. What goes up and down stairs without moving?

34. Many have heard me, but no one has seen me, and I will not speak back until spoken to. What am I?

35. A window cleaner is cleaning a window on the top floor of a 25-floor sky-scraper when, suddenly, they slip and fall! They have no safety equipment and nothing to soften their fall, yet they are not hurt. How can this be?

36. What two superheroes play on a softball team?

37. Mr. and Mrs. Smith have seven daughters. If each daughter has a brother, how many children do Mr. and Mrs. Smith have?

38. Spell *ghost* out loud. Then spell *most* out loud. Then spell *roast* out loud. What do you put in a toaster?

39. I know a word; six letters it contains. And yet if you take one away, twelve is what remains.

40. Which vehicle is spelled the same forward and backward?

41. When you write this time of day in capital letters, it is the same forward, backward, and upside down. What time is it?

42. What word looks the same upside down and backward?

43. What is a seven-letter word containing thousands of letters?

44. I'm tall when I'm young and short when I'm old. What am I?

45. What body part is pronounced as one letter but written with three, and only two different letters are used?

You'll need a calculator for the next three:

46. Think of a number.
    Key it into the calculator.
    Double it.
    Add 10.
    Halve it.
    Subtract the number you started with.
    What number are you left with?

47. Key in the first 3 numbers of your phone number (NOT your area code).
    Multiply by 80.
    Add 1.
    Multiply by 250.
    Add the last 4 digits of your phone number.
    Add the last 4 digits of your phone number again.
    Subtract 250.
    Divide the number by 2.
    Recognize the number?

39. Dozen(s) 40. Racecar 41. NOON 42. SWIMS 43. Mailbox 44. Candle 45. Eye 46. 5
47. It's your phone number.

48. How much dirt is in a hole that's 4 feet wide, 4 feet long, and 4 feet deep?

This is a trick question you will have to ask somebody else, because it only works when said out loud:

> Ask, "There are six teacups on a table. If one falls off, how many are left on the table?"

> Answer: Five. (They will say "59" because they heard you say "60 cups." But you actually said, "Six teacups.")

48. None. There is no dirt in a hole. All the dirt has been removed. The calculator was only a distraction.

Riddle Me This   **215**

NOTES

1. The American Academy of Pediatrics, *Caring for Your School-Age Child: Ages 5 to 12*, ed. Edward Schor (New York: Bantam, 2004).

2. Jonathan Catherman, *The Manual to Manhood: How to Cook the Perfect Steak, Change a Tire, Impress a Girl & 97 Other Skills You Need to Survive* (Grand Rapids: Revell, 2014), 100.

3. This research, which was conducted by the German Society of Ophthalmology, was reviewed in "Women Cry More than Men and for Longer, Study Finds," *The Telegraph*, October 15, 2009, http://www.telegraph.co.uk/news/newstopics/howaboutthat/6334107/Womencrymorethanmenandforlongerstudyfinds.html.

4. "8 Fascinating Facts about Tears," Berkeleywellness.com, accessed February 1, 2017, http://www.berkeleywellness.com/self-care/preventive-care/slideshow/8-fascinatingfacts abouttears#.

5. Sameer Hinduja and Justin W. Patchin, *State Bullying Laws*, Cyberbullying Research Center, updated January 2021, http://cyberbullying.org/Bullying-and-Cyberbullying-Laws.pdf.

6. Jeff Kinney, *Diary of a Wimpy Kid* (New York: Amulet Books, 2007), 4.

7. Amy Poehler, "Harvard University 2011 Class Day Speech," May 25, 2011, https://www.youtube.com/watch?v=7WvdxgGpNVU.

8. Tim Radford, "Secrets of Human Hair Unlocked at Natural History Museum in London," *The Guardian*, May 27, 2004, https://www.theguardian.com/uk/2004/may/27/sciencenews.research.

9. "Water, Sanitation, and Environmental-Related Hygiene," Centers for Disease Control and Prevention, accessed February 1, 2017, https://www.cdc.gov/healthywater/hygiene/index.html.

10. Information taken from Roy F. Baumeister and John Tierney, *Willpower: Rediscovering the Greatest Human Strength* (New York: Penguin, 2011); and Kathleen Vohs, Joseph Redden, and Ryan Rahinel, "Physical Order Produces Healthy Choices, Generosity, and Conventionality, Whereas Disorder Produces Creativity," *Psychological Science* 24, no. 9 (September 2013).

11. Aliciamarie Rodriguez, "US Woman with 42-Foot Fingernails Breaks Record for Longest Ever," Guinness World Records, Longest Fingernails on a Pair of Hands Ever (Female), August 2, 2022, https://www.guinnessworldrecords.com/news/2022/8/woman -with-42-foot-fingernails-breaks-record-for-longest-ever-711160.

12. John Medina, *Brain Rules: 12 Principles for Surviving and Thriving at Work, Home, and School* (Seattle: Pear Press, 2008).

13. Emily Graham, "Fun Principal Incentives to Motivate Students," PTO Today, December 6, 2022, http://www.ptotoday.com/pto-today-articles/article/614.

14. Harry S. Truman Quotes, Truman State University, http://www.truman.edu/about /history/our-namesake/truman-quotes/.

15. Jeffrey Kluger, "The New Science of Siblings," *Time*, July 10, 2006, http://content .time.com/time/magazine/article/0,9171,1209949-2,00.html.

16. "Mirror Twins: Fascinating Facts about Mirror Image Twins," Twin Pregnancy and Beyond, http://www.twin-pregnancy-and-beyond.com/mirror-twins.html.

17. "Sleep in Adolescents (13–18 Years Old)," Nationwide Children's Hospital, http:// www.nationwidechildrens.org/sleep-in-adolescents.

18. Kelly Wallace, "Teens Spend a 'Mind-Boggling' 9 Hours a Day Using Media, Report Says," November 3, 2015, https://www.cnn.com/2015/11/03/health/teenstweensmedia screenusereport/index.html.

19. A. Weinstein and M. Lejoyeux, "Internet Addiction or Excessive Internet Use," *American Journal of Drug and Alcohol Abuse* 36, no. 5 (September 2010): 277–83.

20. Tim Notke, quoted in David Klein, "Hard Work Beats Talent . . . ," By David Klein, May 17, 2021, https://www.bydavidklein.com/2021/05/17/hard-work-beats-talent/.

21. The Olympic Museum Educational and Cultural Services, *The Olympic Games in Antiquity* (Lausanne: The Olympic Museum, 2013), https://stillmed.olympic.org/media /Document%20Library/OlympicOrg/Documents/Document-Set-Teachers-The-Main -Olympic-Topics/The-Olympic-Games-in-Antiquity.pdf.

22. E. A. Kramár et al., "Synaptic Evidence for the Efficacy of Spaced Learning," NCBI, *Proceedings of the National Academy of Sciences of the United States of America* 109, no. 13 (March 2012): 5121–26.

23. W. E. Hockley, "The Effects of Environmental Context on Recognition Memory and Claims of Remembering," *Journal of Experimental Psychology: Learning, Memory, and Cognition* 34, no. 6 (November 2008): 1412–29.

24. Henriette van Praag, "Exercise and the Brain: Something to Chew On," *Trends in Neuroscience* 32, no. 5 (2009): 283–90.

25. Fred R. Shapiro, ed., "Abraham Lincoln," in *The Yale Book of Quotations* (New Haven: Yale University Press, 2006), 466, italics added.

26. Hugh Jackman, interview with Rollo Ross, "That Awkward Moment When Hugh Jackman Remembers He Taught You at School," YouTube, https://www.youtube.com /watch?v=yj46BWpxFcA.

27. Victoria Shannon, "15 Years of Text Messages, a 'Cultural Phenomenon,'" *New York Times*, December 5, 2007, http://www.nytimes.com/2007/12/05/technology/05iht -sms.4.8603150.html.

JONATHAN CATHERMAN is the author or coauthor of multiple bestselling books, including *The Manual to Manhood* and *The Manual to Middle School*. An award-winning writer and sociologist, he is the recipient of the President's Volunteer Service Award, Martin Luther King Jr. Drum Major for Service Award, and multiple Parents' Choice Awards. Jonathan serves his community by mentoring emerging leaders and speaks worldwide about the principles and strengths that empower greatness in children, tweens, teens, young adults, and families.

ERICA CATHERMAN is the coauthor of *The Girls' Guide to Conquering Life* and *The Girls' Guide to Conquering Middle School*. She has spent more than 25 years mentoring young women as a coach to middle school, high school, and college students. Committed to raising up the next generation to be confident, capable, and kind, Erica has served as a youth group leader, community volunteer, and advocate for family health and wellness. She is a certified Yoga Alliance and Group Fitness instructor.

CONNECT with JONATHAN and ERICA

TheCathermans.com